Immortali

John Leslie is University Professor Emeritus of Philosophy at the University of Guelph. A Fellow of the Royal Society of Canada, he was the British Academy–Royal Society of Canada Exchange Lecturer for 1998. He has been Visiting Professor in the Research Department of Philosophy, Australian National University; in the Department of Religious Studies, University of Calgary; and in the Institute of Astrophysics, University of Liège. His publications include *Value and Existence* (1979), *Universes* (1989), *The End of the World: The science and ethics of human extinction* (1996), *Infinite Minds* (2001), and the edited volume *Modern Cosmology and Philosophy* (1998). He is also a contributor to a number of other books, and has authored numerous academic articles.

Immortality Defended

John Leslie

Blackwell Publishing

BLACKWELL PUBLISHING
350 Main Street, Malden, MA 02148-5020, USA
9600 Garsington Road, Oxford OX4 2DQ, UK
550 Swanston Street, Carlton, Victoria 3053, Australia

First published 2007 by Blackwell Publishing Ltd

1   2007

Library of Congress Cataloging-in-Publication Data

Leslie, John, 1940–
Immortality defended / John Leslie.
    p. cm.
Includes bibliographical references (p.   ) and indexes.
ISBN 978-1-4051-6203-6 (hardback : alk. paper) — ISBN 978-1-4051-6204-3
    (pbk. : alk. paper)   1. Immortality (Philosophy)   I. Title.

BD421.L47 2007
129—dc22
2006034424

A catalogue record for this title is available from the British Library.

Set in 10/12.5pt Minion
by Graphicraft Limited, Hong Kong
Printed and bound in Singapore
by C.O.S. Printers Pte Ltd

The publisher's policy is to use permanent paper from mills that operate
a sustainable forestry policy, and which has been manufactured from
pulp processed using acid-free and elementary chlorine-free practices.
Furthermore, the publisher ensures that the text paper and cover board
used have met acceptable environmental accreditation standards.

For further information on
Blackwell Publishing, visit our website:
www.blackwellpublishing.com

CONTENTS

PREFACE

A book about immortality? A book about *God*, therefore? Of the three varieties of immortality discussed here, only one has a firm link to any idea of God, and it alone has a clear right to be named *immortality*. It is the immortality of an afterlife, of thoughts after bodies had died.

Of the other two, the "Einsteinian" variety – the immortality of your existing "back there along the fourth dimension" when people called you dead – is accepted by most of today's physicists, yet the majority of them (and maybe Einstein as well, although he talked of it when comforting the relatives of a dead friend) would hesitate about using the word "immortal." And the remaining variety – being part of a unified cosmic reality that, living the lives of all conscious beings, will live new ones after yours has ended – would be classified by many folk as "not immortality at all."

Does the book truly bring in God, or does it just talk of a Creative Principle in which Plato believed, plus an infinitely rich reality which it created? Did Spinoza acknowledge God's reality when he embraced Plato's Principle and pictured our universe as produced by it? Was he indeed *a pantheist* who thought everything divine? Or was he instead the atheist that many philosophers have described, a trickster who wrote "*God-also-known-as-Nature*" when he actually accepted only Nature? The "Platonistic," "Spinozistic" cosmos pictured in the following pages is infinite in its riches, yet whether to call it "pantheistic" could be entirely a matter of taste. *Atheistic* and *a denial of God* are the words that many would use of it. But nothing much hangs on mere words.

ACKNOWLEDGMENTS

Immortality Defended could not have been written without the help, spread over nearly 40 years, of the editors and the referees of the journals, the multi-contributor volumes, the book series, etc., in which many of its ideas were first outlined. The ideas then sustained thorough testing with the aid of all who went into print with their reactions or took time to send me letters and emails. I am particularly grateful to the editors and referees of the *American Philosophical Quarterly, Mind, Philosophy,* and *Religious Studies.* To Nicholas Rescher, who welcomed *Value and Existence* – my first large-scale defense of a Platonic creation story and of the world-picture which that story suggests – into the Library he was editing for Blackwell. (In the philosophical climate of those days, the theory that the world's existence *is due directly to its goodness* might have shivered for years without a publisher, let alone one of Blackwell's stature.) To Richard Stoneman and Adrian Driscoll at Routledge, who accepted first my *Universes,* with its chapter entitled "God," and next *The End of the World: The Science and Ethics of Human Extinction,* with its sections attacking theories such as make one see no point in trying to save humankind. To Peter Momtchiloff of Oxford University Press who liked *Infinite Minds,* in which various of my present themes are defended in much technical detail. To Anthony O'Hear who took under his wing two of the lectures, "Our Place in the Cosmos" and "The Divine Mind," from my tour as the British Academy–Royal Society of Canada Exchange

Lecturer. (For the first of these, O'Hear had the nice comment that he wanted the new millennium's first issue of *Philosophy* "to start with a Big Bang.") To the editors of Blackwell's encyclopedic *A Companion to Metaphysics* who invited long entries on such topics as COSMOLOGY and FINITE/INFINITE, and then also a startlingly brief one on WHY THERE IS SOMETHING: something rather than nothing, that's to say. To Macmillan for asking me to edit *Physical Cosmology and Philosophy*, and to Prometheus who later published an expanded version named *Modern Philosophy and Cosmology*. Most recently, to all at Blackwell's who have made *Immortality Defended* a reality. They are headed by Nick Bellorini, senior commissioning editor for philosophy.

The book owes a great deal to many others as well, for inspiration and for active encouragement over the years. They include Leslie Armour, Ian Crombie, Ronald Hepburn, David Lewis, Terence Penelhum, Richard Swinburne, and J. J. C. Smart. Also Hugo Meynell whose doubts about my Platonic creation story helped me toughen up my defense of it, and J. L. Mackie whose praise mingled with quite different doubts drew widespread attention to the story as *Value and Existence* had presented it. Despite the doubts, Mackie wrote that it provided "a formidable rival" to traditional theistic accounts of why the world exists. Then again, there was Derek Parfit who had recommended *Value and Existence* to Mackie's attention. He later gave it some influential support, writing that he could find no conceptual flaw in its Platonic maneuvers.

Full enthusiasm for such maneuvers – for saying that an ethical or "axiological" need for a deity or for a cosmos *could by itself explain* the presence of that deity or that cosmos – has come from A. C. Ewing, but unfortunately he died before we could do more than exchange letters. From Nicholas Rescher, too, in his *The Riddle of Existence* and *Nature and Understanding*. From John Polkinghorne whose Gifford Lectures, printed as *The Faith of a Physicist*, held that God-as-a-divine-person might well owe his existence to his eternal ethical requiredness. From Hugh Rice whose *God and Goodness* viewed God not as a person but as the principle that the world exists just because that's good. From Keith Ward whose pantheistic views have become very close to mine.

Updating philosophical idealism with the aid of modern analytical techniques, Peter Forrest and Timothy Sprigge have worked impressively on the nature of consciousness. It was Sprigge who sparked today's debates over why there is something it feels like to be you or me.

(Presumably *being a digital computer* wouldn't feel like anything.) Sprigge's *The Vindication of Absolute Idealism* places him among the greatest philosophers of recent times. Book-writing was a pleasure when people like him could agree with me on so many things.

In addition, the book makes use of many people's ideas in philosophy of science and in cosmology. Here my guides have included Albert Einstein and D. C. Williams; their thesis that the world *exists four-dimensionally* is basic to my description of immortality in one of its three forms. Others have been Bernard Carr, Brandon Carter, P. C. W. Davies, Jacques Demaret, G. F. R. Ellis, Richard Gott, Werner Israel, John Polkinghorne (who, like David Lewis, read right through *Universes* when it was still in typescript), and Martin Rees. Also Michael Lockwood, whose *Mind, Brain and the Quantum* may come as close as anything to explaining why there's something it feels like to be human. However, Lockwood has strong competition in Ian Marshall, Roger Penrose, and Abner Shimony.

I thank the University of Victoria for welcoming me into its philosophy department when I retired to Canada's west coast.

For many reasons, the book owes most to my wife Jill.

Chapter 1

PANTHEISM: A RAPID INTRODUCTION

A Platonic Answer to Why Anything Exists

Imagine that the entire cosmos – every single existing thing – suddenly faded away. In the resulting emptiness, what creative factor could there be? What could bring new things into being?

Even when all things had vanished, countless matters would be *real*. For a start, there would be the reality that the cosmos had existed. There would be no evidence for this because evidence consists of things (records, traces) and those would all have disappeared. But it would be true that a cosmos had been in existence and that you had formed part of it. When once you had come to exist, nothing could destroy the fact that you had existed.

There would also be the fact, truth, reality, that apples and butterflies and clouds, together with infinitely many other objects, were *possibilities* in the technical sense that (unlike round squares) they involved no contradiction. Even dragons would be possibilities in this sense. There would be the fact that if twice 2 clouds were ever to exist in the future, there would then exist 4 clouds. There would be the fact that 3 groups of 5 butterflies, were those ever to exist, would contain as many butterflies as 5 groups of 3. There would be countless other mathematical realities although no things remained in existence.

Might it not be real, too, that the absence of all things was better than something that could have been there instead, a world consisting just of

1

miserable beings? Couldn't it be genuinely the case, necessarily and eternally, that a world of people in mental and physical agony would be worse than no world at all, so that in a situation empty of all people and objects it would be a fact, a reality, that the continued non-existence of the world of agony *was needed or required*? Not required *morally*, because morality concerns good and bad actions; and if all people had vanished, who would be there to act? Still, required in a way we could call "ethical." Covering all of what is good or bad, Ethics deals with more than just moral and immoral behavior.

In a blank, we could then say, a situation including no actual existents, there would be *an ethical ground or reason* for a world of miserable people *not* to exist. Its non-existence would be really and truly fortunate – ethically needful – although there was nobody to be aware of this. Hence the blank would be something of a blessing, in one respect at any rate.

This brings us to Plato. Looking at mathematical, ethical, and other facts about possibilities, Plato concluded that they were necessary and eternal facts. He denied that they were created by the thoughts we have about them. And Plato had a theory about why the cosmos exists. A situation empty of all existing things, while it might be something of a blessing in the way just now explained, would be unfortunate as well, because something better might have been there instead. In the emptiness there would be a ground or reason for a good cosmos to come to exist, for its presence would be required ethically. Now, Book VI of Plato's *Republic* tells us that The Good "is itself not existence, but far beyond existence in dignity and power" since it is "what gives existence to things."

The ethical need or requirement for the existence of a good world is not, in other words, something that can become real only when there already exists some actual person or object. It is too much "beyond existence" for that to be so. But, the Platonic suggestion runs, the actual world of people and objects is a good one and *it exists simply because it ought to*. Its ethical requiredness – the fact that there is an ethical need for it – *is itself creatively effective*. If seeking "what gives existence to things" we need look no further.

Plato is not saying insanely that all ethical requirements are always fulfilled, let alone that they are fulfilled just because they truly are *requirements*. By definition of the word "bachelor," no bachelor can be a bigamist. By definition of "husband" every husband has one wife at least. In contrast, a definition of "ethically necessary or required" could never guarantee that ethical necessities or requirements were always satisfied. It couldn't even guarantee they were satisfied in at least one case: for instance, the case of a divine mind whose existence was supremely good, ethically needed in a fashion that could never be over-ruled by stronger ethical needs. Nothing in the sheer meaning of such terms as "good" or "required ethically" could ensure that a divine mind existed or that the world did not consist solely of miserable people. The Platonic theory could make sense only as a speculation, not as something whose correctness could be demonstrated by mere logic or by a dictionary.

Pantheism: The World's Patterns are Nothing But Divine Thought-Patterns

Can Plato's theory survive, though, even as a speculation? Surely the sole things the theory could explain would be ones that were very good indeed. The most plausible candidates for being explained on Platonic lines would be minds perhaps worth calling *divine*, minds that con-templated ("knew," "thought about") absolutely everything worth con-templating. If ethical necessities could ever by themselves create anything, would not minds of this sort be the very first things to be created? And why would anything less good ever come to exist? Why is there the world we actually see?

One solution is the *pantheism* developed by Spinoza, who lived from 1632 to 1677. A natural way of interpreting him is as follows. There is a divine mind, a mind whose reality is due to the eternal ethical need for it. We, like all the other intricately structured things of our universe, exist merely because the mind in question thinks of this universe in all its details. The universe's highly intricate patterns would in any event have been present, necessarily and eternally, among the possibilities available for the divine mind's contemplation, for they were not like the patterns of round squares. But being contemplated in all their intricacy has made them more than merely possible. It has made them patterns of genuine existence, because a vastly intricate divine universe-picture is what the universe *is*. Apart from divine thinking there exists nothing whatever.

When, Spinoza saw, a very intricate pattern is pictured in its every detail, then a pattern with that degree of intricacy certainly must exist, a pattern carried by the mind which does the picturing. Any pattern that a mind carries is an actually-existing pattern, obviously, and not a merely-possible pattern. Now, how could a mind picture every detail of an intricate pattern *while itself carrying neither that pattern, nor anything structurally similar to it*? That could be thought worse than magical. It could look as bad as any round square. (Structural similarity can be rather hard to define – but do not expect a chess computer to analyze a complicated chessboard situation without mirroring that situation inside itself, constructing something similar in structure for its information-processors to work on!) A highly complex arrangement of hugely many elements could not fail to be real inside a divine mind when such a mind's thoughts extended to hugely many universe-fragments organized in a highly complex way. It would be real there, not illusory, whether or not any similar arrangement could be found in *some other* system of elements *external to* the mind in question. And if Spinoza's pantheism is right, there is no such "other system of elements" – no universe-pattern actually in existence outside divine thoughts themselves.

The point is that Spinoza sees no charms in the theological doctrine that God is Pure Being unstained by anything so vulgar as structural intricacy. Convinced instead that any divine mind thinking of vast structural complexities must be vastly complex in its structure, he views our universe as just part of such a mind's structure.

Physics is not hostile to this. Physicists describe the world's structural details instead of saying, uselessly, that it is made of "good, solid stuff, nonmental and nondivine." No experiment could reveal that the physical world existed outside a divine mind, not inside one.

True, virtually all philosophers used to insist that minds were entirely different from all physical objects, for example brains. Every mind had properties wondrously mental. Each brain was crudely material. Any idiot could see, they thundered, that minds could not possibly be brains, or even parts or aspects of brains! However, such thundering is far less common today. But are we now to thunder instead that no physical universe could ever be a part or aspect of any mind, even a divine one? Why ever should we?

Consider "eidetic" imagery. Suppose somebody, gazing up at a blank ceiling, "saw" (in an experience that seemed just like looking at the real thing) a slide-rule such as every engineer carried before pocket calculators were invented, and then performed accurate calculations through willing its central bar to slide to and fro. Wouldn't you conclude that *mental structures* and *physical structures* need not be so very different? Well, those blessed with eidetic imagery truly have calculated accurately with slide-rules vividly "seen." Again, they have proved able to fuse (as if by placing one transparency on top of another) two eidetically remembered sketches of such things as waves, smoke, clouds, this letting them detect such new things as a face whose lines had been "encoded" by being shared between the sketches. If mental states could never contain structures like those of slide-rules, sketches, and so forth, then how could such feats be possible?

Sure enough, we fail to be aware that we and our surroundings are simply patterns of divine thinking, as on Spinoza's theory. But why should we be aware of it? How ever could we be?

Remember that Spinoza views us as only very tiny elements of divine thoughts: very tiny parts *of God* if we choose the word "God" to name the cosmic mind that "thinks our universe into existence." Picturing rocks and trees in absolutely all their structured intricacy, would this immensely intricate mind be picturing things that thought they existed as parts of it? Certainly not, for rocks and trees do not themselves think anything. The rocks and the trees would exist as parts of it nevertheless, because intricately structured divine thought-patterns would be what they were. Now, when such a mind formed its fully detailed ideas of you and me, we'd again be things existing as parts of it, but in this case the things would themselves have thoughts. They would be strictly limited thoughts, however, since those are all that humans ever have. Doing a lot better than rocks and trees, humans are still far from omniscient. They could be very tiny constituents of God's reality without automatically knowing it.

Agreed, whatever strictly limited thoughts were had by us humans would be divine thoughts as well as being human thoughts, because they would be elements of a divine mind. They could be extremely limited nonetheless. They could sometimes be entirely mistaken thoughts. They could include the thought that Spinozistic pantheism was obviously wrong. Some might actually be the thoughts of convinced atheists. People who formed part of God's reality would not be ejected from it just as soon as they turned atheist.

However, isn't there the difficulty that divine thought-patterns would have to be unchanging? For if a divine mind existed because of its goodness, its ethical requiredness, why on earth would it ever alter? Why would it ever contemplate anything except the total of all that was worth contemplating? Wouldn't any changes in it be changes for the worse?

Time and Eternity

Spinoza's answer to the problem of Time – of how Change can exist if our intricate universe is nothing but intricately structured divine thinking – has attractions for many scientists. It helps explain why Albert Einstein admired Spinoza's world-view.

Spinoza did write that God, with an existence that is due to its perfection, *cannot change*, because unable to change for the better. And yes, he declared that apart from God there exists absolutely nothing. But does this say that our world's unceasing variations are illusory? Not in the least. Even if all its events are "eternally there," our world can include variations of a sort, somewhat as a block of wood can – for successive cross-sections of the block can differ from one another. Einstein wrote that his theory of relativity made it "natural to think of physical reality as a four-dimensional existence instead of, as hitherto, the evolution of a three-dimensional existence." A tadpole growing into a frog may be not too unlike a road starting off narrow outside Los Angeles but growing broad before reaching San Francisco. When humans become more and more decrepit with the passage of the years, their deterioration could be interestingly similar to that of a railway line which gets more defective with each additional mile of its passage across Canada.

In a divine mind, *thinking* and *being a mind* would be rolled into one. Such a mind would not need to generate its thoughts. It would eternally possess them all, or rather, it would itself be those thoughts joined together in an unchanging whole. But pantheists who said this would not be denying changes of the sort accepted by Einstein when he discussed things moving relative to one another.

Pantheism and the World's Imperfections

If our universe in all its intricacy is intricate divine thinking, why are our lives so unsatisfactory? Why is God not thinking about something much better?

A possible answer is that God truly is thinking about something much better. God is thinking about that *also*. In addition to thinking of all the structure of our universe, God thinks of the structures of immensely many other universes. All those universes exist inside the divine mind quite as much as ours does (for here, instead of meaning Absolutely Everything In Existence, "universe" is just a label for a gigantic, well-integrated collection of entities; hence "many actually existing universes" isn't a contradiction like "monogamist with many wives"). The divine mind contemplates everything worth contemplating. Our universe is among the things worth contemplating, but maybe it is far from the best of those things.

The divine thoughts might well extend to many items *not* organized into universes. God might think of all possible chess moves, and of all possible moves in innumerable board games superior to chess. God might contemplate all possible beautiful paintings, symphonies, and artworks of types that humans have never dreamed of. God could perhaps contemplate lives that began inside physical universes but stretched onwards *outside* them, which is what many people have in mind when they talk of *surviving the deaths of their bodies*. The most a pantheist need claim is (*i*) that our universe is somewhere among the things worth thinking about, things contemplated by a mind that contemplates everything worth contemplating, and (*ii*) that it is a universe worth thinking about in all its details.

That is to say, divine thoughts about our universe are better through not having ragged gaps. They include knowledge of exactly how it feels to be a Plato or a Spinoza writing great philosophy, but also of how it feels to be a Hitler with a severe toothache and formulating vicious plans. Saying that humans formulate and carry out plans does not deny that they are elements in divine thinking. What if the intricately structured lives of those humans are just intricately structured patterns inside an infinitely complex mind? The plans are formulated and carried out nonetheless.

7

Pantheists might well argue, however, that divine thoughts did not cover every single truth about possibilities. God could well fail to contemplate just how it would feel to suffer all possible torments in all possible universes, and in situations too disorderly to be called universes. And while perhaps contemplating not only the truth that 2 and 2 made 4, but also *the truth that it was a truth*, and maybe even *the truth that it was a truth that it was a truth*, God might avoid contemplating all the infinitely many other truths that continue this sequence. Again, the divine ideas mightn't extend to every page in the dreadful Library of Babel imagined by J. L. Borges, filled with all possible book-length permutations of the alphabet's letters. While it would be an eternal fact that those permutations were all of them possible, God might be God without thinking about this fact in all its details which would mean considering every single permutation.

Suppose that divine thinking did need to extend to all the details of all possibilities. We could then be forced to reject pantheism on the following grounds. Of the innumerable universes that (unlike round squares) involved no actual contradictions, hugely many would be scenes of utter chaos. Furthermore, universes that had been orderly for billions of years could themselves become chaotic at any moment. It would be conceivable that people in such universes suddenly turned into blackberry jam. They could suffer disasters of this sort without joining law-abiding criminals, vegetarian cannibals and habitually drunk teetotallers. Now, *the range of ways* in which such disasters could conceivably occur *is vastly greater* than the range of those in which they could fail to occur, because at every instant countless matters could conceivably go wrong. So if God contemplated in full detail absolutely all things that could be contemplated in full detail – all that truly could be conceived without contradiction – and if the reality of your life and mine were simply, as pantheists believe, the reality of God's thinking about various of those things, then ought we not to expect each moment to be our last? Shouldn't we expect to turn into jam, burst, softly and suddenly vanish away, or whatever?

Unified Consciousness

A divine mind would be unified by something more than just the interactions of many separately existing parts. Such a mind's knowledge would be immensely complicated in its structure. However, the structure would be formed from elements that were no more truly separate in their existence than the red "part" and the blue "part" of the color purple, or the "element" of a brick which is its length and those other "elements" which are its width, its shape, and its solidity.

That, at any rate, is the standard view among theologians. The divine mind would be no mere collection. It would be *a single existent*. And something very similar has commonly been taught about the nature of every mind, and above all about human minds (or regions, at least, inside human minds). Although consciousness of a complicated scene includes many thousand distinguishable elements, it could be perverse to view these as united solely by their causal interactions. For if that truly were the case, how could our mental lives have any more intrinsic worth than the goings-on inside modern computers? (While a computer's information-processing can bring benefits to us, surely no computer of today has a mental life worth living.) And anyway, don't we all know that it isn't in fact the case, whenever we are conscious of some complex scene in all its thousands of parts? Is it in the least plausible that groups of transistors, or cogwheels, or ropes and pulleys performing computations through interacting in the right fashion, could have consciousness like yours or mine?

In effect, it seems we know by direct experience that at least some parts of our universe – our own minds, or various regions inside them – possess the kind of unity to be expected in a pantheistic scheme of things. They have many distinguishable elements, all influencing one another intricately like the soldiers of an army or the transistors of a computer. However, the existence of each element is never fully separable from that of the others.

Although believing that our universe's parts are elements of something *unified in its existence*, pantheists would never claim that this was evident at a glance. The various bits of the universe are not utterly mashed together! Even if all of them are aspects of a single existent, some bits are much less closely, less obviously linked than others. Inside a divine mind that knew everything worth knowing there could be countless lesser minds like yours or mine, each knowing very little. Still, such knowledge as they had would often be of elements that fairly evidently *weren't* completely separate in their existence. You have knowledge of this type when conscious of your own thinking. Anything worth calling *a thought* has to be a combination of many ingredients, but any human thought has a degree of unity not found in any thought (if we can call it that) whose ingredients are the activities of silicon chips in a computer you could buy this week.

Some people view such ideas as in conflict with modern science. In point of fact the reverse is true. Quantum theory indicates that many parts of our universe, and perhaps all of them, definitely are not fully separate in their existence. In order, for instance, to estimate the probability that two elementary particles are in different halves of a box, quantum physicists must treat those particles as sometimes each of them in the left half *and also* in the right half. A unified reality, so it seems, can be in two places at once.

Unity and the Infinite

If the Platonic creation theory is correct, then the unified complexity of a divine mind could be expected to be far greater than the complexity of just a single universe. The divine thoughts would presumably be far better if extending to the structures of countless universes. True enough, the divine mind described by Spinoza appears to have contemplated one universe only. But, with multiple universes featuring so frequently in the theories of twenty-first-century scientists, it would be strange if twenty-first-century pantheists set such limits to the divine reality. Why shouldn't divine thoughts extend to infinitely many universes, perhaps obedient to infinitely many different laws of physics? All the universes might exist as elements of a single mind's thinking when that mind was divine.

On the other hand it could be wrong to theorize that Reality in its Entirety formed a single existent. For if it were supremely good for a mind to contemplate all that was worth contemplating, then why ever – against the background of Plato's account of creation – would there exist just the one mind of this sort? Wouldn't it be far better for there to be infinitely many such minds, each separate in its existence from the others? Or suppose that this were impossible on the grounds that minds each contemplating everything worth contemplating *would possess precisely the same properties*, and that (which is very controversial) *possessing precisely the same properties* is a nonsensical idea. Wouldn't there then be one mind that contemplated absolutely everything worth contemplating, plus innumerable other minds each failing to contemplate some tiny triviality that was contemplated by all the others?

To see the force of this last point, imagine that there exists a mind infinite *in negative value*, maybe through being filled with infinitely much undiluted suffering. Could it make sense to say that the coming to exist of a second mind that was equally awful *would be in no way tragic*, just because the existence of the first mind was in itself infinitely tragic? Could we deny any need to annihilate the second mind, even if we lacked all other means of terminating its agony? Surely not. But why, then, would anyone say that the existence of a mind infinite *in positive value*, a mind that contemplated everything worth contemplating, would leave Platonic ethical requirements with nothing else they could usefully create? How could it be thought that a second mind of the same kind would not add to the excellence of the situation? If there did exist infinitely many minds, each of infinite worth, would it be quite all right to annihilate all but one of them, just for fun?

As pantheists, we might best use the word "God" to refer to a divine mind in which our universe is contained. Thinking that there existed infinitely many further minds of the same kind, we could then call these "other deities." Still, we might instead prefer to use "God" as a name for the entire infinite collection.

Too Good to be True?

Helping itself to such terms as "divine" and "pantheism" in a controversial way – for (as the Preface noted) "a denial of God" is what many would instead say here – this book will defend a pantheism of infinitely many divine minds, each contemplating everything worth contemplating. As indicated earlier, that could be very different from contemplating absolutely everything, for a great many matters (such as exactly how it would feel to suffer all conceivable agonies) might not be worth thinking about. Still, each mind could presumably be infinite in the sense that it had infinitely many thoughts. Just thinking of every pebble in an infinite line of pebbles would involve being infinite in this sense.

Since scientists are not in the business of deciding whether the world's patterns are patterns of divine thinking, none of this could conflict with the findings of science. But all the same, wouldn't accepting it be like believing in Father Christmas? Wouldn't it be too incredibly good? Not if Plato's theory of creation makes sense, for on this theory Reality's goodness must presumably be infinite; yet does Plato's theory in fact make sense? Could *the sheer ethical need for a thing* ever manage to explain its actual existence? The next chapter will look at the matter in detail.

Before the present chapter ends, though, let us agree that acceptance of a Platonic and pantheistic world-picture wouldn't be "belief in Father Christmas" through seeing the world as a cozy place, without dangers. If our universe is among the things meriting a divine mind's contemplation, what is contemplated in this instance is a universe obedient to physical laws. If any danger-averting miracles occur in it, then only extremely rarely.

One way of looking on the affair is as follows. Despite how miracles could prevent them, our world contains many disasters. If trusting the Platonic answer to why anything exists, we must view it as a world where the need for various disaster-preventing miracles *is overruled* by other needs: for example, by the need for the kind of interest possessed by a world obeying physical laws everywhere. There is still a genuine need – an ethical requirement – for disasters not to occur. That's implied, after all, when you call events "disasters." Now, decent folk *try to bring this need into line with* any need for miracles to be absent. By what means? By doing their best to prevent disasters, of course! Nothing in pantheism denies that people have minds of their own, minds that are directed sometimes towards producing disasters and sometimes towards preventing them. The next chapter will look at this point as well.

One disaster we should try to prevent is the extermination of the human race in the fairly near future. In *The End of the World* (subtitled "The Science and Ethics of Human Extinction") I discussed a "doomsday argument" first stated by the mathematician Brandon Carter. Just as it could seem absurd to view our intelligent species as *the very first* of many million that were destined to appear in our universe, so also it could seem preposterous to fancy that you and I are in a human race almost sure to spread right through its galaxy, a process which could well be completed in under a million years if germ warfare or other perils failed to kill everyone before the process started. It could seem preposterous because, were the human race to spread right through its galaxy, then you and I would presumably have been among the earliest millionth, and very possibly the earliest billionth, of all humans who would ever have lived. It might be far more sensible to view humankind as quite likely to become extinct shortly unless we take great care. Now, pantheism has nothing whatever to say about all this. It does not tell us that if we fail to take the care then divine thinking will (for example) "think germ warfare out of existence." Being a world inside a divine mind is fully compatible with being a world of germ warfare or of something still more deadly such as – see the first of the two Technical Notes below – a scalar field disaster. Why have we discovered no extraterrestrials? Perhaps because intelligent species almost always destroy themselves soon after developing advanced technologies.

Technical Notes

(A) Disastrous upsetting of a scalar field which is "merely metastable," like a statue balancing upright but only precariously, has been examined in major physics journals. A quick discussion, "Premature Apocalypse?," appears on pages 205–7 of *Before the Beginning* by Martin Rees – Astronomer Royal – who warns that "caution should surely be urged (if not enforced)." See also pages 108–22 of *The End of the World* and the various articles I cite there. It is generally thought that elementary particles get their masses through interacting with one or more scalar fields, the word "scalar" signaling absence of the kind of directionality that makes magnetism detectable by a compass needle. Any such field might be like a ball wanting to roll downhill but trapped in a hollow. A violent enough shove could "knock the ball out of the hollow." Maybe a collision taking place inside some physicist's particle accelerator could give the shove. So far, the greatest energy densities known to us are those of colliding cosmic rays which can sometimes pack the punch of rifle bullets into extremely tiny regions. However, Steven Weinberg has suggested (*Dreams of a Final Theory*, chapter 10) that collisions inside particle accelerators might one day rival head-on crashes not just of rifle bullets but of small jet aircraft! If the ball were then knocked out of the hollow, an initially microscopic bubble of new-strength scalar field would expand at almost the speed of light with enormous release of energy. It would destroy not merely Earth but our entire galaxy, and next all the neighboring galaxies, etc.

(B) Brandon Carter's doomsday argument is sometimes challenged as follows. Suppose there were vastly many intelligent extraterrestrials scattered through space and time. Wouldn't an observer's chances of being *a human living around AD 2000* be virtually unaffected by whether most humans lived at much later dates, thanks to the human race spreading right through its galaxy? Unfortunately the argument survives the challenge. The crucial point is that we ought (until we find enough contrary evidence) to try to see ourselves as "fairly ordinary" inside the various classes into which we fall – bearing in mind, naturally, that in some cases there might be tradeoffs to be made because being more ordinary inside one class might involve being less ordinary inside another. Now, you and I fall not only into the class of *observers* but also into that of *human observers*. And a human observer, finding that the year is near AD 2000, can picture himself or herself as *fairly ordinary among human observers* through supposing that the human race *isn't* destined to spread right through its galaxy. Were humankind to become extinct shortly then, because of the recent population explosion, something approaching a tenth of all humans would have lived when you and I did.

Notice that even if humans were statistically very unusual among all observers scattered through space and time, observers falling into vastly many different species, there might still be nothing too odd in being a human rather than a member of some other intelligent species. Suppose, for instance, there were a trillion intelligent species all of exactly the same population size. Being a human would then put you in the one-in-a-trillion bracket; but so would being a Martian or just anything else, and therefore it would be no oddity. In contrast, it would be strange to be a very unusually early member of whatever intelligent species you found yourself in.

Further Reading

Spinoza's pantheism is developed in his *Ethics* and in his earlier *Short Treatise of God, Man, and His Well-Being*. Although far the less famous of the two books, the *Short Treatise* is in many ways the better of them since the *Ethics*, eager to provide firm proofs of everything, can seem to describe the world as a product of mere logic.

Hegel gave new twists to many of Spinoza's ideas, more being added by F. H. Bradley (*Appearance and Reality* is his best-known work) and other British Hegelians of the late nineteenth and early twentieth centuries. A very competent modern defender of Spinozistic and Hegelian themes is Timothy Sprigge, in *The Vindication of Absolute Idealism*. Plato's theory about why the world exists has been extremely influential – when you appreciate that Spinoza and Hegel accepted it, a great deal of what they wrote can begin to seem sensible – yet Sprigge develops his position without its aid.

Plato's theory comes as a shock to many philosophers trained in the tradition of British, North American and Australasian philosophical analysis. A. C. Ewing, however, was working inside that tradition when his *Value and Reality* used a Platonic approach to explain the existence of a divine mind – but not the divine mind of pantheism. In *God without the Supernatural*, in contrast, Peter Forrest is attracted both by a Platonic creation story and by a pantheistic world-view. For my own earlier, rather complicated efforts to defend these two things, see in particular *Value and Existence* and *Infinite Minds*. The pages now in front of you try to show that Platonism and pantheism supply a thoroughly straightforward answer to why the world exists, when technicalities are set aside.

For further modern work on pantheism (or on "panentheism," a name some-times given to any theory saying that the divine existence contains much in addition to a universe or set of universes) consult *In Whom We Live and Move and Have Our Being*, editors Clayton and Peacocke, which concentrates on pantheistic Christianity. Pantheism is also central to much Hindu thought: see the *Upanishads* in particular.

David Lewis, formidably skilled at philosophical analysis, argues for a scheme of things which may contain considerably more than mine does. His *On the Plurality of Worlds* maintains that everything conceivable, including the Greek deities, can be found in some world or other.

Numerous writers see quantum theory as describing complex wholes in which, as in Spinoza's universe, there are no parts existing separately from one another. One of them is the physicist David Bohm: consult *The Undivided Universe*, for instance. Another is the philosopher Michael Lockwood, of *Mind, Brain and the Quantum*. Lockwood argues that items in our conscious states are fused together in ways which quantum physics can explain. Also that when, for example, we experience a few musical notes in swift succession, items separated in time are themselves fused in those ways, showing that the world does have "a four-dimensional existence" as suggested in the fifteenth edition, enlarged, of Einstein's *Relativity: The Special and the General Theory*.

In *Our Final Century*, Martin Rees devotes a chapter to Carter's doomsday argument. He sees no actual way of refuting it. Over several years of looking at it, I may have found ways of reducing its force, but that's all.

Later pages will have more to say about the above-mentioned sources. The Bibliography at the end of the book lists most of them, yet not the works of early writers like Plato and Spinoza since these are available in so many different editions and translations.

In his latest book, *Pascal's Fire*, Keith Ward develops ideas markedly similar to mine. However, he argues for just a single infinite mind.

Chapter 2

PLATONIC CREATION

The Good of Plato as a Creative Principle

"The Good is what unifies, orders and sustains the world." – The words are from Plato's *Phaedo* and the theory that they express is developed by Socrates, who acts as Plato's spokesman. I cited Plato's *Republic* as giving us some insight into the theory and in particular into its claim that The Good, identified as "what gives existence to things," is "itself not existence." Plato holds that innumerable facts are independent of all of the things of our world. Instead of being human inventions, countless realities (mathematical, ethical, etc.) are real necessarily and eternally. It is among them that we must look when trying to explain the world's presence, he thinks. At least on the matter of their necessary and eternal reality, he would seem to be right.

Take the fact that, in contrast to a round square, a world like ours could exist without contradiction. This would be a fact even if nothing at all existed. To become a fact, a reality, it would not been forced to wait until some world actually sprang into being or until people developed languages in which things could be described without contradiction. On the contrary: if there ever was a time at which our world had not yet come to exist, then its chances of doing so would themselves have depended on how it wasn't like a round square. Again, suppose 4 groups of 3 roses came to exist in some garden, making 12 when folk counted them expertly. The mathematical reality met with here – that any 4 groups of 3 things, *were they ever to exist*, would always include exactly twelve things – wouldn't have depended on the actual existence of anyone expert at counting, or of any roses or other countable objects.

Similarly with ethical truths. That any world filled with interest and happiness *would indeed be better* than one filled with boredom and misery – well, how unconvincing it could be to classify this as something that could not be real until, say, the actual arrival of people able to evaluate things, or of stars and planets, or of a Big Bang in which a universe burst into being!

Plato becomes distinctly controversial, however, when he theorizes that The Good "gives existence to things" or, as I'd express the point, that the ethical requiredness of the cosmos is what accounts for its existence. Even to professional philosophers it sometimes comes as a huge surprise that anyone would defend such a view today. Among those trained in the British, North American, and Australasian tradition of philosophical analysis, the standard opinion is that nothing could possibly account for the existence of the cosmos. It must exist for no reason whatever.

All sorts of criticism can be brought against Plato's attempt to see things differently. And he says so very little in defense of his theory that some folk read right through his works without noticing it. Instead of realizing that Plato thought he could say why the world exists, they come away only with a vague impression that The Good somehow reigns supreme among those mysteriously abstract realities, the Platonic Forms.

Why wasn't Plato more talkative on this topic? Maybe it was because the reality in which he believed, that an ethical ground for the existence of the cosmos had itself been creatively sufficient, was an extremely simple one. If it did not at once strike others as something in which they, too, might believe, something quite as credible as the alternative that the cosmos exists for no reason whatever, then efforts to paint it in attractive detail could be self-defeating. When something truly is simple, it has few or no details to be painted.

Possibly, again, it was because he was little interested in defending the excellence of the cosmos as shown to us by our senses, for he maintained that our senses deceive us rather badly. And possibly it was because he would have shuddered at various objections that philosophers now often treat as decisive. The objection, for example, that the goodness of a possible world cannot be a creative factor, seeing that to call something good "merely expresses a favorable attitude towards it instead of genuinely describing it."

Modern objections like that will be considered in due course. Let us first look at some respects in which Plato's theory has been influential.

God as a Creative Principle; God as a Creating Person; or God as the Entire Cosmos

Over many centuries, the idea *that The Good itself acts creatively* appears again and again in Neoplatonic writings. Here two main themes are typically developed side by side. (A) First, all things that exist in time and space, "temporal things" for short, are subordinate to a realm of eternally existing entities, the Forms described in Plato's *Republic*. These somehow place their imprints on everything that is merely temporal. Following a perhaps very unfortunate suggestion of Plato's, it is often held that the Forms alone are fully real. Anything temporal can have only a shadowy existence. Our five senses may seem to assure us that a river or a hill is very real indeed, yet they are feeding us with illusions. Still, they are reliable enough to reveal instances where one and the same Form puts its stamp on two or more things, as when the Form of The Red is made manifest in all red objects. (B) Next, the Form of The Good is responsible for the existence (to the extent that this isn't illusory) of the world spreading itself before us in space and in time.

In the works of Neoplatonists, the Form of The Good – "The Good" for short – tends to be identified with *the divine*. Since the Form is understood to be (as Plato said) "itself not existence" but "far beyond existence in dignity and power," this doesn't at all mean that an eternally existing divine person created everything beyond himself. Instead, the very nature of goodness makes it eternally and necessarily true that there is a need, an ethical requirement, for the cosmos to exist, and *this need itself* is what wields creative power.

Isn't such a theory refuted when we find only a few billion years separating us from the Big Bang? Perhaps not. The Big Bang is nowadays often viewed as a mere episode in the career of a cosmos that has

18

always existed. Besides, Einstein's writings suggest that there is a good enough sense in which all existence is eternal existence.

At any rate, Plato's basic point is sufficiently plain. No matter whether its temporal extent is finite or infinite, the world at every moment owes its reality to The Good. If we are to talk of God at all, then God can be identified as a creative factor, force, or principle. God, we could say, is *the Platonic truth that the ethical requiredness of the world is itself responsible for the world's existence.* Or God is *the world's creative ethical requiredness,* or perhaps *a creatively powerful ethical requirement for the world to exist.* These are simply alternative ways of phrasing the same point. The word "God" may be defined slightly differently in each case, but the imagined situation is always the same.

That some factor "created" the world need not mean that initially no world existed and then the factor suddenly became active. Theologians call the world "divinely created" because they think God responsible for its existence whether or not it has existed eternally.

Writers thinking along Neoplatonic lines may include LEIBNIZ. See, in particular, his *The Ultimate Origin of Things.* In one of its passages, at least, this pictures competing goods as struggling for existence, much as loads linked by pulleys each struggle to move downwards. The greatest possible descent of weight then results automatically, without the intervention of any conscious agent.

PLOTINUS can definitely be included. In his *Enneads* Plotinus claims that "The Good on which all else depends" is something that itself "has no need of Being." Our world therefore exists "by sheer necessity" rather than as the result of a judgment by some divine planner. It nevertheless has a structure by which any such planner "would not have been disgraced." Look, too, at DIONYSIUS, who declares in *The Divine Names* that the creative cause of all existing things "does not take thought" when generating the world, since it itself is "what is not." It is not an existent, in other words. Consequently it cannot be a thinking, planning person.

Again, the *Guide for the Perplexed* of MAIMONIDES says that the only positive attributes we can ascribe to God are "attributes of action." Instead, then, of picturing some Designer and Creator, it would seem better to understand the divine reality as a matter of creative energy.

Particularly common in the Greek Orthodox church, this theme is found also among Protestants and Catholics. Paul TILLICH insists that

God is "the Ground of Being" rather than a mere being. Hans KÜNG maintains that God, although definitely a reality, is still "not an exist-ent" of any kind, and thus "not a supramundane being." With an eye on such things as the *Commentary on Aristotle's "Peri Hermeneias,"* which describes God as "outside the realm of existents, as a cause which pours forth everything that exists," some contend that AQUINAS thought likewise.

Inside the modern analytical tradition, the same general approach has been taken by Nicholas RESCHER (who, however, prefers to talk of "an axiological principle" or "principle of what's for the best," avoid-ing the words "God" and "ethical requiredness," which strike him as suggesting a divine person with a moral duty to create a world). Also by Hugh RICE, for whom the statement that God acted creatively says merely that the world exists "because it is good that it should"; we must reject the picture of God as "a concrete *something* which wills and cre-ates." Then too, there is Derek PARFIT. While himself feeling that the world's evils may make all such notions too hard to accept, Parfit has at least written that best-ness would be "a plausible selector." By this he means, he explains, a factor which "selects what reality is like" and is such that we could reasonably believe that, if reality did turn out to have the selected properties, then this "would not merely happen to be true." For Parfit, the idea that the world has "creative ethical requiredness" – that, as he rephrases the point, "there is a best way for reality to be" and that this "explains *directly* why reality is that way" – cannot be dismissed as logical or conceptual nonsense.

Note, though, that later passages in Leibniz's *The Ultimate Origin of Things* can appear to portray God as somebody whose decrees brought all other things into existence. What Leibniz actually believed was as follows, I think. A supremely strong ethical requirement, formed when innumerable lesser requirements all came together compatibly, is what generated the cosmos in its entirety. It is a scheme of things with a divine person as by far its most important element, the center around which all other entities are organized.

Some writers believe, in contrast, that only a divine person's existence is due directly to its ethical requiredness, everything else existing simply through the divine will. DESCARTES is among them. True, he defends an Ontological Argument which at first glance runs as follows. God, being by definition perfect, cannot fail to exist, because the concept of actually existing (or, in one version of the Argument, the concept of having *necessary existence*) enters into the concept of possessing perfection, much as the concept of wifelessness enters into that of being a bachelor. The affair is a simple question of the meanings of words! However, a careful reading of him shows that he relies on what he sees as God-given insight into the reason for the divine existence, not on mere definitions. In his *Replies to Objections* he insists that "a word's implying something is no reason for that thing's truth." His real position is therefore probably close to that of such modern authors as A. C. Ewing, Keith Ward, and John Polkinghorne. EWING views himself as only spelling out what so many religious thinkers have in mind when they suggest that God's perfect goodness and God's reality are intelligibly linked. "God's existence," he declares, can be necessary "not because there would be any internal self-contradiction in denying it but because it was supremely good that God should exist"; "the hypothesis that complete perfection does constitute an adequate ground of existence does seem to be the only one which could make the universe intelligible and give an ultimate explanation of anything." WARD, writing as Oxford's Regius Professor of Divinity, states that of course a thing's ethical desirability never leads to its existence in a fashion provable by logicians, but "if there is something which, as Aristotle has suggested, cannot exist otherwise than it does, the best reason for its existence would lie in its supreme goodness." (ARISTOTLE declares in his *Metaphysics* that "the cause of all goods is The Good itself" and that God, the First Mover, "exists necessarily, and inasmuch as he exists by necessity his mode of being is good.") POLKINGHORNE considers that God may well be "self-subsistent perfection" in which cause and effect come together in "the creative effectiveness of supreme ethical requiredness."

Finally, Plato's central idea – that an ethical need could itself act creatively – has sometimes been given a pantheistic turn. The God of SPINOZA (like Brahman in the Hindu *Upanishads*, writings that Erwin SCHRÖDINGER considered in agreement with those of quantum theorists) is a divine mind that includes all reality. This mind, "*natura naturata*," exists through a principle of goodness, "*natura naturans*." In his *Ethics*, Spinoza tells us that God-alias-Nature "has an absolutely infinite power of existence," for "perfection does not prevent the existence of a thing, but establishes it." He had said earlier, in his *Short Treatise*, that God's nature was such that no change in it could possibly improve it, and that "through his perfection, God is the cause of himself." Greatly influenced by Spinoza, HEGEL comments that the cosmic "Idea which thinks itself," an entity which "embraces all characteristics in its unity" and so is "The Absolute and all truth," is one in which "The Good is really achieved." "The Idea," he explains, "is not so powerless as to possess a mere right to exist without actually existing."

It is now high time to consider typical modern protests against Plato's attempt to place The Good at the world's foundations. Let us concentrate on the theory that creative ethical requiredness – ability to exist simply because of being good – is something had by the entire cosmos, the set of all existing things. This, though, is just for simplicity's sake. For points in defense of such a theory could apply equally to the view that the requiredness is had solely by a divine person, the creator of everything else.

Initial Objections to the Platonic Theory

(*i*) How, for a start, could something as abstract as *the ethical requiredness of a cosmos* ever do anything, let alone act creatively?

This can seem to call for a very short answer. Anything able to create an entire cosmos, a sum total of all existing things, would of course have to be "abstract" in the sense that it did not depend for its reality on the prior existence of any of those things. It would have to be a Platonic reality, necessarily and eternally real. That's not an objection to Plato's theory. It *is* Plato's theory.

"But [the inevitable protest comes] no abstract facts can ever themselves influence the world!" – What, can't they? Toss a coin 10 times. While you might get 10 heads, various rather abstract facts make you 10 times more likely to get just one. Or consider the puzzle in which 15 numbered squares slide around inside a larger one into which 16 could fit. Half the seemingly possible rearrangements of the 15 squares are in fact impossible. Abstract mathematical requirements combine to force this. Or take the fact that three 5s are 15. If 3 groups of 5 lions go into a wood and only 14 lions come out, think twice before entering the wood!

Certainly the concept of being ethically marked out for existence, ethically necessary or required, contains nothing about influencing the world. It isn't one and the same concept as that of being marked out *causally or creatively*. But an ethical necessity or requirement still manages to be analogous to a causal necessity or requirement (for instance, that some iron bar will have to move towards a magnet) in the following respect. It is something fulfilled, satisfied, when the required entity, activity, or state of affairs has actually come to exist. While this cannot prove Plato right, it may at least give him a chance of being right.

(*ii*) Many philosophers call themselves "emotivists" or "prescriptivists" in Ethics. Some things really are good, they say, and others really are bad, but they do not here see themselves as describing realities. For emotivism, "really good" and "really bad" are in the same camp as "Hurrah, and I really mean it!" or "Boo, and I considered this thing's characteristics truly carefully before booing it!" For prescriptivism, calling an act "really good" is a matter of prescribing it (emphatically and on mature reflection) together with all sufficiently similar acts. On both theories there are no ethical requirements "really out there in the world" in the way that seas, ships, and sealing-wax are really out there, or that mathematical realities (for instance, that 3 sets of 5 cats are required to include 15 cats) are really out there. Hence Plato's theory fails at once.

The short answer is that emotivism and prescriptivism fail to capture what people ordinarily mean when maintaining, for example, that feeding hungry children is good. As theories of good and bad, emotivism and prescriptivism may be rather too like declaring that humans are ripe melons or that a beast could deserve to be called a dragon although it could not fly, didn't breathe flames, and had no tail or scales or claws. The same applies to ethical relativism. This holds that things can indeed be good or bad, but only relative to particular systems for evaluating them. All such theories appear to forget that, while everything in this area might perhaps be as fictitious as dragons, the ideas of right and wrong, good and bad, were formed by people who were doing their best to describe realities beyond those of how humans reacted to various deeds or situations. They could then classify all who rejected their ethical opinions as benighted folk, persons sadly mistaken about the world, instead of just as folk who favored different things.

Remember that ethical prescriptivism talks not of describing any realities of good and bad, but of prescribing actions. It has proved remarkably popular. Ask yourself, though, how its defenders could possibly say many things we'd ordinarily want to say: for instance that it was good that conditions on our planet allowed intelligent life to evolve, or that the suffering of animals was bad long before moral agents arrived on the scene. Just which deeds could be being prescribed here? Just who could be being asked to do them?

(*iii*) More generally, when anyone holds that all ethical necessities are really only needs for *people already in existence* to act in particular ways, and hence could not conceivably explain the existence of absolutely everything, then the short answer is that the field of the ethically necessary – of what *ought to exist* not purely hypothetically, in contrast to hydrogen bombs which "ought" to be among your possessions if you want to destroy all life on Earth, bombs "good" for that purpose – extends far beyond the requirements *of morality*. All sorts of things (for example, the evolution of intelligent life) could be genuinely fortunate, truly good, without being good deeds, moral actions; and calling them good can be more than just another way of saying that people ought to favor them. The goodness of a thing – of an entity, activity, or state of affairs – isn't a quality added to its other qualities like a coat of paint, but neither need it be simply how the thing stands with regard to moral agents. It can be a status the thing has, the status of being called for, marked out for existence, in a fashion which is no mere matter of somebody's duties with respect to it or, let us add, of some strange duty of its own. If you dislike using the word "ethical" when talking of needs which are not needs *for action*, feel free to substitute some philosopher's word such as "axiological" whenever I write about "ethical" needs; but please never assume that by "ethical" I must always mean *moral*! Suggesting that the world *exists because it ought to exist*, Plato is not making the crazy proposal that it exists because it had a moral duty to.

(*iv*) Cannot we protest, though, that Platonic ethical requirements could never be verified experimentally? Where do people's ideas of good and bad come from, after all? Isn't it from how their societies try to encourage particular ways of behaving by imagining requirements "out there in the real world"? So when calling various things "genuinely good," shouldn't all sophisticated thinkers really mean that their societies do pressure them to prefer such things?

The short answer is that this would be like really meaning, when you said dragons genuinely existed, that your society did want you to believe in dragons.

Suppose it were completely obvious that goodness and badness, ethically required existence and ethically required non-existence, could never be verified. Why should this be crucially important? Imagine Mr. Jones just sitting there, doing nothing, on the grounds that it could not be verified that other behavior was better. Picture Mr. Jones failing to escape from flames, or making no effort to move a baby out of the flames, on those same grounds. Would it not be a sign that he needed mental treatment? Besides, whether a thing can be verified is seldom a clear-cut affair, to the disgust of the philosophers who made "verifiability" the test of what's meaningful. There would be nothing too wrong in saying that the approach of the flames "was all the verification a sane person could ask" for the need to move the baby.

It could conceivably be that nothing in the world was ever genuinely good or bad. If that were true, there would then be no real point in believing it true, because there'd be no real good or avoidance of real bad in anything whatever. Still, I'd hesitate to say I *knew* it wasn't true. Yet couldn't we justifiably hospitalize people who considered it true? Couldn't we reasonably view them as dangers to themselves and to others since they didn't think along lines that were ethically necessary?

Compare the case of what philosophers name "the Problem of Induction." It concerns our inability to produce evidence that the future is likely to resemble the past in various respects: for example, in that cuts and bruises will continue to cause suffering. David Hume thought it entirely question-begging to argue that, because people using past experience as a guide to the future *had in the past* been generally successful, they would probably be successful *in future*. But if Hume was correct, so what? Hume never doubted how silly it would be to reject the guidance of experience. Thinking such things as that bruises will continue to cause suffering *is required rationally*. And failing to think in rationally required ways – repeatedly picking up red-hot iron, perhaps, because you said you couldn't produce evidence that the past was any guide to the future – would earn you a place in a mental hospital. Well, similarly with thinking or failing to think in ways required ethically. If your standards of verification made you seriously doubt whether the death of a baby in a fire was something bad or whether trying to prevent famine was ethically demanded, you would need hospitalization.

25

If the Platonic Approach is Correct, Why Struggle to Produce Good Things?

"All the same, isn't it plain that the cosmos cannot be a product of Creative Value? If it were, where would be the point of moral efforts? Wouldn't the presence of all good things be guaranteed automatically, and the absence of all bad ones?"

What such an objection apparently overlooks is that genuine needs could compete with one another. They could overrule one another. If it failed to embody this idea – if it called the cosmos "perfect" in the sense that every ethical requirement was always satisfied – then Plato's theory would be ludicrous.

Look at what people have often said about a divine person. He is described as omnipotent. In other words he can do anything except create spherical cubes, rocks too massive for him to lift, supremely worthwhile states of agony, and suchlike. Well then, why doesn't he prevent plague or genocide or even little acts of meanness? Why doesn't he produce beauty and happiness everywhere? Mustn't it be irrational to worship his supposed goodness? A theologically traditional answer is that, while excellent reasons do exist for divine intervention in the world, they are *overruled* by still better reasons. It is suggested, for instance, that we could not be free, or at least not with freedom of the sort the divine person rightly gave to us, were ours a world of constant divine interference: evil deeds punished at once by lightning strokes, fires always extinguished before they became life-threatening, paintings of great beauty appearing out of thin air. Suggestions on these lines surely make enough sense to rescue the divine person's worshippers from plain irrationality. Why on earth would things be any different when that person was replaced by a Platonic creative principle? When Plato suggests that ethical requirements are themselves responsible for the existence of our cosmos, he need not be telling us to expect ethically guided thunderbolts, flames that take care never to harm anybody, superb artworks popping into existence everywhere.

Some believers in a benevolent creator persist in protesting that there are (to quote words sent me by one of them, Hugo Meynell, a leading philosopher of religion) "no known parallels in our experience to ethical requiredness of itself giving rise to actual states of affairs." "In the world as we know it" (Meynell continues) "such requiredness only counts as a reason for the existence of something when there is a conscious agent able and willing to act in accordance with it. Thus I might reasonably be confident that a restaurant did not serve substandard food, or that a school did not teach palpable fictions as though they were facts, if I had grounds to believe that the restaurateur or the headmistress were competent, intelligent, and virtuous people." Yet why do those generating such protests judge their own theory immune to obvious variants on them? For a start, are they not convinced that an omnipotent deity would constantly step in to enforce good behavior or to set things right, if and whenever such intervention would be good? However, no stepping-in is evident in the world as we know it. So does this not indicate that omnipotent benevolence is a fiction?

"Not at all," comes their answer. "It would be bad if humans were puppets compelled always to behave in admirable ways. It would be bad if our lives were filled with miraculous stepping-in." What is more, they then typically add, we must consider (1) the universe's grandeur; (2) the fact that it is an intelligible universe, a puzzle our minds can unravel, as is shown by the spectacular success of the natural sciences; (3) the law-abiding elegance of its causal sequences, which constant miracles would destroy; (4) its life-permitting properties, suggestive of careful divine choices; and (5) the sheer fact that it exists. These things might all reasonably be taken as signs of a divine person's power and benevolence. – Very good; but why cannot a Platonic creation story include entirely similar points?

Why cannot the Platonist believe that ethical requiredness "of itself giving rise to actual states of affairs" has done whatever a benevolent deity would have? Why cannot the grandeur, the intelligibility, the law-abiding elegance, the life-permitting properties, the sheer fact that there is a world and not a blank, be viewed as evidence that some ethical requirements are themselves creatively successful? We actually experience all these things. Considered as a possible item of evidence, each runs parallel to the others. How much force, then, can there be in the complaint that there are "no known parallels in our experience" to ethical requiredness itself producing anything real? And if the non-fulfillment of various needs – for the existence, say, of up-to-standard restaurant food – is any argument against the Platonic account, why does it not throw equal doubt on the competence, intelligence and virtuousness of a divine creator?

Very true, any signs we may have of the productive power of ethical requiredness are not as uncontroversial as our evidence that some folk are virtuous agents, for the grandeur of the universe, its intelligibility, its life-permitting properties, etc., are not supplemented by such miracles as rotten potatoes turning into fine ones when the bad restaurateur adds them to the stew. But is the productive power therefore absent from "the world as we know it"? Well, how are we to handle those slippery words? Atom bombs were absent from "the world as the cavemen knew it," but were atoms too? (The cavemen knew the world. It was a world of atoms even in their day. Still, *in a sense* there were no atoms "in the world as they knew it.") Are quarks, are superstrings, absent even nowadays from "the world as physicists know it"? (We may have signs of their existence, but only controversial ones.) And, granted we *don't know* that our world was God-created, must we conclude that "the world as we know it" *wasn't* God-created?

Then again, are there any "known parallels in our experience" to a deity who exists for no reason whatever? (The ethical requirement that he exist is infinite in its intensity, Meynell thinks, but good heavens, this does nothing to explain why he exists. He just *is*, entirely reasonlessly.) Or to a deity having power – also for no reason whatever – to cause worlds to spring into being by mere decrees or acts of will? And by the way, isn't it very standard theology that the world continues to exist and to obey its physical laws *only through the divine will*? Magnets never attract iron "just of themselves," hammers never drive nails through a power entirely inherent in them, according to numerous theologians. Now, how strange to accept this happily yet at the next moment be amazed by the Platonic suggestion that the world continues to exist and to obey its physical laws *only through this being ethically required*!

To be sure, people do not always do what is ethically required of them. But remember, it is central to the Platonic creation story that not every ethical requirement is a moral requirement, a need for good behavior. It follows that those ethical requirements *that are* needs for good behavior can be in constant danger of entering into conflict with other ethical requirements *that aren't*, namely, the ethical requirements that (according to the Platonic story) have created our universe, making it one in which people can themselves decide whether to behave well or wickedly, without miraculous interference. Good people are then those doing their best to ensure that no conflict occurs. The good restaurateur makes efforts to keep awful things out of the stew. What if success crowns those efforts? In that case any ethical needs that had created a universe in which the restaurateur was no puppet *wouldn't clash with* – and so would have no chance of *overruling* – any ethical need for up-to-standard food to be served. A bad restaurateur may act differently but this cannot refute Plato.

Platonists who are pantheists may be particularly well positioned for tackling this area. They need not even claim that our world – unprovided with ethically guided thunderbolts, self-constructing cathedrals of immense size and beauty, miraculously well-run restaurants – is a world of the very best possible variety. They need only view it as one of countless worlds that deserve a divine mind's contemplation. Also they can avoid any problem of why a divine person, instead of using his omnipotence to create innumerable minds each of infinite richness, chose to produce realities that were nothing like as fine. Chose to produce them, that is to say, not just as patterns of his own thinking but as things external to himself.

How Creative Power might be Real Necessarily

We could be better positioned for judging the force of Plato's theory if some deity had equipped our minds with immensely strong ethical searchlights – but presumably that is an outdated fantasy. Again, it could help if a thing's goodness were a matter of logic. This would be so if dictionaries told us that labeling something "good" meant it had qualities (pleasurableness, for instance) drawn from a specified list and combined in accordance with specified rules. Like mathematicians investigating what follows from standard definitions of "line," "number," or "division," we could then calculate the consequences of the rules. We could hope to work out whether Schopenhauer was right in calling the world's existence an ethical disaster. But unfortunately the word "good" never behaves like that. We cannot settle ethical disputes by feeding dictionary definitions into computers.

Still, surely there must be *good-making qualities*, no matter how hard it is to know which they are. When something is self-justifying – when its existence is ethically required for its own sake – then the thing's qualities make it just the thing that it is, and they also make it intrinsically good; but how? What firm necessity can link the qualities to the goodness?

J. L. Mackie considers this puzzle in *The Miracle of Theism*, and earlier in *Ethics: Inventing Right and Wrong*. Now, he recognizes that the ordinary idea of a thing's intrinsic goodness is the Platonic one. It is ordinarily believed that entities, activities, or states of affairs with various natural qualities (ones in principle detectable by scientists) possess the Platonic "nonnatural quality" (or, as I might prefer to say, *status*) of having an existence that is ethically required. Their requiredness, people think, is not purely relative to the tastes of particular individuals or societies, neither can it be known by consulting dictionaries. Yet while finding no contradiction in any of this, Mackie considers it much too bizarre. How, he asks, could anything's good-making qualities be firmly linked to its goodness, if not by logic? But without a firm link, wouldn't it be possible for the things of one world to be good while those of a second world, like those of the first in all their qualities, were entirely lacking in goodness? – which would be absurd, as he rightly comments. His conclusion is that goodness in the ordinary sense of the word must be as fictitious as any dragon. Goodness was "invented" to help societies to control their members.

It is easy to avoid such a conclusion, though, for why should anyone think that the only firm necessities are logical necessities? Logical necessities follow directly from how words or other symbols are defined ("Every bachelor is necessarily unmarried"; "Anybody with a cousin must also *be* a cousin") or else can be proved by linguistic or symbolic maneuvers based on definitions ("A bachelor with an unmarried cousin must himself be an unmarried cousin"). Well, why fancy that only necessities of that type can set limits to what is genuinely possible?

Take the case of similarities between the afterimages produced by bright lights. Here we avoid the problems raised by differences between how things seem and how they really are. If an afterimage seems to be colored red, then red is how it really is colored, in the sense of "colored" that applies to afterimages. These have what is called "phenomenal color." Now, a blue afterimage, a purple afterimage, and a red afterimage stand in firmly dictated relationships. Every blue afterimage is necessarily nearer in color to a purple afterimage than to a red one. And this is no mere consequence of defining purple with the words "bluish-red." Cavemen without languages could see that blue afterimages just had to be more color-similar to purple than to red ones. It is because such different degrees of similarity truly do exist, independently of all definitions, that any definition of purple as *bluish-red* can be understood.

If you feel uncomfortable with the case of afterimages, consider the more general point Bertrand Russell made repeatedly when discussing what philosophers call "Universals," which are at least roughly the same as the Forms described by Plato. Russell concluded we could never manage without all Universals because thought and language have to rely on the Universal *Similarity* (or *Resemblance*). Well, without launching into a long discussion of what Universals are, of the part played by them or by their near equivalents in Plato's thinking, or of whether *Similarity* truly is one of them, let us just note the main matter Russell was drawing to our attention. Thought and language would be impossible unless various things were, initially and in themselves, specially much alike in various respects which languages could then pinpoint by using one and the same word in each case, perhaps the word "blue" or the word "bluish." Their alikeness could not fall away from the things while these remained unchanged, like a rope falling away from two planks it had bound together. It would be present with a completely firm necessity.

Now, when it seems so clear that completely firm necessities can go beyond all logical necessities, ones guaranteed by definitions of words or other symbols, what excuse could Mackie have for fancying that any necessity that wasn't a mere matter of logic would be *too bizarre* to link a thing's goodness to its other qualities? No excuse at all, so far as I can see. His rejection of goodness in the ordinary sense – ethical requiredness of a kind that is necessarily "out there in the world" independently of social pressures – rests on the alleged oddity of any absolute necessity that is not merely logical. And yet when you look at his position closely, doesn't Mackie himself accept a necessity of precisely this kind?

Recall that Mackie views the ordinary idea of goodness as picking out something that is logically possible. Possessing such goodness is not like being a triangular circle. Goodness of the sort believed in by ordinary folk is something whose absence from the world is not logically guaranteed. It follows that if it really is (as he thinks) absent from the world, then this must be a matter either of chance *or of some necessity that isn't logical*. But he does not see chance as active here. Remember, he very rightly denies that the things of one world could be good while those of another world, like those of the first in all their qualities, were entirely lacking in goodness. From which it follows (and why ever did he fail to notice it?) that in this area we are dealing with a nonlogical necessity, one way or the other. Goodness as commonly believed in, an ethical requiredness linked to ordinary, scientifically detectable qualities, either (*a*) is present in the world with a necessity that isn't a logical necessity, or else (*b*) is absent from the world, once again with a necessity that isn't a logical necessity. Hence the sheer fact that its presence would involve a nonlogical necessity could hardly make it "bizarre."

Similar comments apply when Mackie moves on from discussion of mere ethical requiredness, looking instead at *creative ethical requiredness*. He accepts in *The Miracle of Theism* that the idea of creative ethical requiredness is central to a tradition stretching back to Plato and that it involves "no actual contradiction." Nevertheless he rejects such requiredness. Yes, he thinks, logic did not forbid a cosmos to exist in direct response to an ethical need for it; but any such need, if it wasn't just a human invention, never actually managed to create anything. In actual fact the cosmos just happens to exist. Well, I ask, could this *actual fact* be something that itself just happened to be the case? Could it be possible for a cosmos of a certain description to be a direct product of its ethical requiredness, while in point of fact such a cosmos chanced not to be there? Presumably not. Presumably Mackie's theory is instead that the absence of creative ethical requiredness is on a par with the absence of mere ethical requiredness, goodness as ordinarily believed in. It is an absence guaranteed not by logic but by something else. *By some nonlogical necessity*, that is to say, although this normally clear-headed philosopher never thought things out sufficiently clearly to say it.

Alternatively, Plato could be right. The cosmos could exist because of being ethically required, with no help from any further factor. While not a matter of mere logic, this would involve a necessity every bit as firm as any logical necessity. There would be nothing evidently freakish here.

Creative Value Would Not Be Something Complex

The two alternatives – that the ethical requirement that there be a cosmos of a certain type *necessarily was* creatively powerful, and that it *necessarily wasn't* – are equally simple. It wouldn't be "straight-forward" if an ethical need for a cosmos remained unfulfilled, yet "unstraightforward" if the need brought about its own fulfillment. Either way, a nonlogical necessity would be operating, and the one situation would be quite as uncomplicated as the other. Neither would involve clockwork whirring, hammers hammering, magnets attracting or repelling, magic wands waving, words of power being spoken, or complex productive or annihilatory forces. Given an ethical need for a cosmos of such and such a kind, nothing would "make" this need *able to bring about its own fulfillment*, but neither would anything "make" it *unable to bring about its own fulfillment*. You might almost as well believe that some magic wand "made" phenomenal blue nearer to phenomenal purple than to phenomenal red, or that a deity's command "made" unvarying misery worse in itself than interestingly varied happiness.

Would it be important that a blank, the absence of a cosmos, would be an utterly simple reality whereas any cosmos at all like ours would be something immensely complicated? Might Plato's theory have been adequate for explaining a little iron sphere, had that somehow managed to be intrinsically good, whereas what we actually find, if it doesn't just exist for no reason whatever, could have come to exist only through planning by some immensely powerful and intelligent person? It is hard to see why. Why should the creative power of ethical requirements come with the limitation, "just so long as what was required wasn't too complicated"? Would anyone argue that to create something complicated a Platonic creative principle would have to be implausibly clever whereas even a *stupid* Platonic creative principle could create a little iron sphere?

As Mackie recognized, people ordinarily think of goodness as an ethical requiredness "out there in reality." It is a status that various possibilities supposedly have, that their existence is what's needed. Now, the ethically required existence of some possible cosmos is either creatively effective or not, these alternatives being equally simple. Mackie fully appreciated that classifying the first alternative as "too bizarre" could not involve accusing it of excessive complexity. The Platonic theory was that our cosmos was a possible cosmos which (unlike, say, one crammed with agony) had ethically required existence, and that this was creatively sufficient *by itself* instead of being important only thanks to complex processes which proceeded successfully.

Granted, though, that the ideas of being ethically required and of being creatively required are two separate ideas, not one, haven't we a right to say that ethical requiredness *as such* would not wield creative power? Well, yes; but so have we a right to say that no cow "as such" is brown – in the way, that is to say, in which cows as such are female while bulls as such are male. The point cannot justify thinking that an ethical requirement could be creatively powerful only if accompanied by clockwork or magnets or magic spells or acts of divine will or feats of intellect.

None of this gets anywhere near a proof that The Good is in any way powerful. Still, an ethical need for a cosmos would at least have various properties essential to any world-generating, world-sustaining factor. For remember, it would not depend on the prior existence of any person or object. If real at all, it would be real necessarily and eternally. And it would be *a requirement for the existence of things* that wasn't just hypothetical, *IFfy-THENny*, like the requirement that there be 20 rabbits *if* there are 2 groups of 10.

Further Reading

The works of Plato, Aristotle, Plotinus, Dionysius, Maimonides, Aquinas, Descartes (for his Ontological Argument, see his *Meditations* and *Replies to Objections*), Spinoza, Leibniz, and Hegel are all available in many different translations and so do not appear in this book's Bibliography, which does list those of the more modern writers mentioned in this chapter: Ewing's *Value and Reality*, for example, Ward's *Religion and Creation*, and Polkinghorne's *The Faith of a Physicist*. For Hegel's ideas, his *Logic* (the first part of his *Encyclopedia of the Philosophical Sciences*) is particularly important.

When they ask whether the world might be the product of an ethical (or "axiological") need for it, Mackie, Parfit, Polkinghorne, Rescher, Rice, and Ward are reacting to my *Value and Existence* or to chapter 8 ("God") of my *Universes*.

Chapter 3

DIVINE AND HUMAN MINDS

Review of the Position

Let us take stock of the position now reached. Recognizing that count-less realities to do with *possible things* are real necessarily and eternally, Plato searched among them for some factor able to explain why our world exists. Mathematical realities – e.g., that if there were ever to be 2 sets of 2 dragons, then there would be 4 dragons – clearly could not be responsible for the actual existence of anything. Ethical realities perhaps could. The absence of a cosmos of undiluted misery could be *required ethically* even in a situation empty of all existing things, and therefore of all people burdened with moral duties to keep such a cosmos out of existence. Similarly, the presence of a good cosmos could be required ethically in that same situation. Might not the requiredness be creatively sufficient by itself, rather than having to be put into effect by some reasonlessly existing deity? If there were no deity, there would then presumably be nothing outside the ethical need for a good cosmos that could "give force to it," nothing to "make" it creatively sufficient; but so what? Necessities can be necessities without anything "making" them necessary. Think of how interest and pleasure could be necessarily better than boredom and misery, or of how experienced blue could be necessarily more like experienced purple than like experienced red. What would "make" these matters necessary? Nothing.

An ethical ground for the existence of some possible world would itself lead to that world's actual existence, or else it would not. Neither of these alternatives would be forced by mere logic, yet neither would be a case of sheer happenstance. There would be a necessity here, one way or the other. Whichever way the necessity was, it would be equally simple. Plato's theory of the world's creation could therefore perhaps be right. Recent analytical scrutiny of it, for example by J. L. Mackie and Derek Parfit, suggests that it is not grounded on conceptual confusions.

People accepting the theory include Plotinus and Dionysius; maybe Maimonides, Aquinas, and Leibniz; and more recently the theologians Paul Tillich and Hans Küng, together with the philosophical analysts Nicholas Rescher and Hugh Rice. All of these suggest that ethical or (as Rescher prefers to say) "axiological" needs are directly responsible for the cosmos in its entirety. The word "God" is then often used as a label for this supposed fact. But there are others (Aristotle and Descartes could be examples, and A. C. Ewing, and such theologians as Keith Ward and John Polkinghorne) for whom God is a person whose existence could be explained by his ethical requiredness, nothing else being explicable in this fashion.

I argued, though, not only that Plato's theory is best used for explaining the entire cosmos – everything in existence – but also that the sole cosmos it could readily explain would be one we might label "pantheistic," a cosmos somewhat as imagined by Spinoza. For suppose that The Good really could act creatively, as Plato believed. Suppose also, as can seem very plausible, that nothing could be better than divine thinking. Why would there exist anything else, then? Well, according to Spinoza there is indeed nothing else. Divine thinking is the only reality. Our intricately structured universe is an intricate pattern in a divine mind.

In fact Spinoza seems to have believed that divine thinking extended merely to a single universe, and he clearly considered such thinking to exist in one divine mind only. What strange restrictions he was placing on the creative power of The Good! Surely divine thought would be far richer if it extended to the structures of countless different universes. And wouldn't the presence of infinitely many minds that we might call "divine" be better than that of just one? Compare how the presence of infinitely many miserable minds, each of immense negative value, would

be *worse* than that of just one – so that we'd have good cause to annihilate as many of them as possible, were there no other way of putting an
end to their misery.

Accepting Plato's answer to why the world exists, we may in effect have
to picture divine minds as present in infinite number. If we continued
to speak of "the" divine mind, this should then be much as islanders who
believe in many islands still talk of "the island" – in other words *theirs*.
We ought to mean "our" divine mind, the one containing our universe.

A Pantheism of Infinitely Many Divine Minds

Let us work on the assumption that things never *just are*, for no reason
at all. Instead, Plato's approach to the world's existence is correct. Consequently there are infinitely many realms of eternal thinking, each so
rich and so unified that we might reasonably name it *a divine mind*,
with absolutely nothing beyond them. You and I, and the universe of
which we are ingredients, must therefore be nothing but patterns contemplated (or "thought about," or "thought into existence") inside one
such realm or mind. Remember (*i*) that physicists tell us only about the
world's structure, the arrangement of its parts, instead of saying it is
composed of "stuff" that is "good and solid and not the stuff of divine
thinking"; (*ii*) that the patterns of many possible universes like ours
could well be things worth contemplating; (*iii*) that any mind worth
calling "divine," unbeatable in its value, must presumably contemplate
absolutely everything worth contemplating; and (*iv*) that when some
pattern of great intricacy is pictured in full detail, then a pattern with
that kind of intricacy must genuinely exist in the mind that does the
picturing, whether or not anything of the sort exists elsewhere as well.

Being worth a divine mind's contemplation may not make our universe the best of all possible universes, or even one that is particularly
good. It could be that innumerable other universes, all of them contemplated as well, were considerably better. The situation is just that ours is
a universe among the countless matters that earn a place in divine thinking. It itself is contemplated by "our" divine mind, the one inside which
you and I exist. But each of the infinitely many other divine minds
must, I think, contemplate a universe exactly like it. If so, then every
such mind will include people who are exact duplicates of you and me.

It might here be protested that no two things, not even divine minds, could be exactly alike in all their properties; or alternatively, that divine minds that differed from one another "would have the good of Variety." Let us take these ideas in turn.

Can two or more things have precisely the same properties? Some philosophers have wanted a Principle of Identity of Indiscernibles that forbids it. For instance, they say, there simply could not be a cosmos consisting of two identical, perfectly homogeneous spheres surrounded by empty space. In *Infinite Minds* I explained why I joined the many other philosophers who reject Identity of Indiscernibles. Here let me just insist that accepting it would not change things very much. Identity of Indiscernibles would not prevent the existence of infinitely many divine minds, each infinitesimally different from all the others – for example through all but one of them being ignorant of a single, utterly trivial fact among infinitely many facts that were worth knowing, a different trivial fact for each mind. Compare the case of two infinitely large universes, the first differing from the second only in the placement of a single atom. Identity of Indiscernibles would have nothing to say against it.

How about Variety, then? Well, the thoughts of a single mind could certainly be better through being immensely varied. But what if each of two minds contemplated absolutely everything worth contemplating? Presumably this situation could not be improved by making one of them contemplate something else.

As was emphasized earlier, contemplating everything worth contemplating could be very different from contemplating absolutely all truths about possibilities. Many such truths could be so uninteresting, messy, or unpleasant as to be not worth thinking about. What value could there be in considering all possible sequences that an eternally typing monkey could type? And why should divine thoughts extend to just how it would feel to undergo all conceivable varieties of torture? And although conscious of the placement of our universe's every electron, mightn't a divine mind fail to be specifically aware of just which electron had most other electrons within 822,976,352 kilometers of it, or within 558,248,237 times the present length of your longest eyelash? Surely its thinking could be unbeatable in its value without having to extend to *that*, let alone to every single way in which every single fact is related to every other fact.

38

Still, a divine mind could not contemplate all of our universe's structure without contemplating a great deal that was unpleasant, or worse. Mayn't this prove pantheism's wrongness?

Some would here appeal to the Privation Theory of Evil. Accepted by Augustine, Aquinas, Spinoza, Leibniz, and numerous others, this maintains that nothing – not even extreme pain – has an intrinsic value below zero. Evil states of affairs are merely of disappointingly low worth. Blindness, for instance, is being unfortunately deprived of the good of sight. Supporters of the Privation Theory can agree with everybody else about what's better than what in the realm of existing things. Where they disagree with most of us is in thinking that none of these things *is in itself worse than utter emptiness.* Can their position be refuted? Presumably not, for intrinsic value is scarcely the sort of reality you could test for in laboratories. However, we can defend pantheism without having to join them. Remember, we can reason that a divine mind's knowledge of a possible universe could well be better through having no ragged gaps – gaps corresponding to such matters as just how it feels to have a toothache.

We can also insist that not even pantheists need approve of everything that happens in the world as we find it, a world without ragged gaps. Saying that everything is part of divine thinking *doesn't* call the cosmos "perfect" in the sense that every ethical requirement is always satisfied. An ethical requirement could fail to be satisfied because it entered into conflict with other ethical requirements, and sometimes the conflict could be something we could rectify. By new actions of ours, we could bring various ethical needs back into line with one another. It could often be our actions that had generated the conflict in the first place, causing, for instance, a clash between (*a*) whatever ethical needs had given us a world in which we were no puppets, without freedom, and (*b*) an ethical need for us to shun embezzlement and murder. Being parts of a system of divine thinking would not render us powerless to influence events. Even in a system of billiard balls set in motion by an expert player, one ball can influence another.

How Humans would Fit Into a Divine Mind

People often find it very hard to grasp that being parts of a divine mind would not make them powerless or give them reason to praise everything that happened. Spinoza himself was far from clear about it. He can be found writing that we should "wait for and bear with equal mind all forms of fortune, because all things follow from the eternal decree of God" – which makes nonsense of his own courageous efforts to improve the world instead of just waiting to see what events took place.

One thing to keep in mind is that pantheists who view each divine thought as eternal, so that our intricate world (which is pictured as nothing but intricately structured divine thinking) must be in some sense unchanging, need not deny that clock-hands move and trains travel across continents. When Einstein spoke of our world as having "a four-dimensional existence" this didn't mean he never looked at a clock in horror and ran to catch a train. The point is a difficult one, for it can at first glance seem self-evident that if catching or not catching the train were "already there, just a little further along the fourth dimension," then there'd be no point in running, since hurry could not affect the affair. The first-glance argument is mistaken, however. Although eternally spread out in a system that existed four-dimensionally, events could still be connected by all the normally recognized chains of cause and effect. In Einstein's world just as in anybody else's, deciding not to run for a train can lead to failure to catch it. Einstein does not deny that anything ever causes anything else. For him as for most physicists, causal patterns are simply patterns conforming to physical equations. The equations can apply to the world just as well, whether or not its existence is four-dimensional.

Philosophers have long struggled with a very similar point when asking whether the world "is fully deterministic" – meaning that like a perfect clock it would go through precisely the same sequences as before, could it but be returned to one of its earlier states. Some have argued that in a world of complete determinism there would be no point in efforts. Either you would be fated to catch the train, or else you would be fated to miss it. No need to run, therefore! However, that's another mistake. Whether the world is fully deterministic is a question for physicists in laboratories, not just philosophers in armchairs. Humans do weigh alternatives, decide between them, and act in ways that make a difference to their surroundings, but so (at a much more primitive level) does any chess computer. Admittedly, the computer fails to possess freedom of a mysteriously absolute type, freedom whose misuse might lead to richly deserved hellfire. Why believe, though, that humans themselves possess such freedom? Again, why view every pantheist as denying the freedom that humans do have?

What follows from all this is that people inside pantheism's cosmos would have all the commonly accepted reasons for trying to improve their surroundings. Being parts of God would not mean they had no influence on the world, let alone that they never could affect it in good or evil ways. They would not be God's puppets, any more than they would have God's knowledge of everything worth knowing. They would have minds of their own, usable for good or for bad.

What would divine knowledge be like, on the pantheistic world-model, and how would human minds be related to it? Covering absolutely everything worth thinking about, divine thoughts would include ones whose intricate structures were the structures of people restricted in their powers, occasionally frightened, ignorant of many things, and so forth. Spinoza recognized this, else his writings would have been a denial of what you and I actually experience. That there are elements of God's reality that are frightened and ignorant is crucial to his theory. But he believed, as well, in a divine overview in which everything was appreciated in a single glance, this overview being present in what we might call *a region of divine personality* characterized by actual emotions: sympathy, for instance, for the hopes and fears of limited and ignorant beings. Spinoza's *Ethics* speaks of how complete knowledge of everything isn't had by God "insofar as he is considered as constituting the essence of the human mind" – in plainer language, in those ingredients of God's intricately structured reality that themselves *are* human minds – but is nonetheless found in God "insofar as he possesses the ideas of all things." The latter element in the divine reality loves individual humans, the love for them entering into "the love with which God loves himself" (for, Spinoza explains, "it is the nature of God to delight in infinite perfection").

Can we have actual evidence for any of this? (*i*) Consider the sheer fact that there is a world and not just an eternal realm of mere possibilities. How on earth could such a fact be explained if Plato were mistaken about why things exist? Plato's theory, however, leads to pantheism for the reason given earlier. Wouldn't divine thinking be the best thing that there could be? Why ever would there exist anything else, were Plato right? So the pantheist asked for "actual evidence" could reply, "Have you overlooked the fundamental truth that a world exists?" (*ii*) There are general features of our universe – orderliness, for instance, of the kind leading us to talk of "causation" and of "physical laws" – which might be explicable only by Plato's theory. These general features, too, could then be counted as actual evidence for the pantheism to which Plato's theory leads. (*iii*) But there could in addition be evidence of a more direct type. The world's events do often appear to have *unity* of a sort to be expected among elements of a divine mind.

Here we reach various difficult questions. Some concern the unity of physical systems as investigated by quantum theorists. Others are about the unity found in our own states of mind.

Unity of Existence, Not Mere Causal Integration

If at all like Spinoza's, any pantheism will insist that the parts of our universe are unified by something over and above mere causal interactions such as give unity of a kind ("structural unity," let's name it) to a whirlpool, to a steam engine, to an ant colony, or to an army. As elements of a divine mind, all the parts would be joined in what can be called "existential unity" or "unity of being." Each would be merely an abstraction from the divine whole, much as a stone's color and its shape are abstractions from the stone. Although not in the least unreal, the color and the shape lack the sort of reality that would permit each to exist in isolation. There could not be "disembodied shapes," shapes not belonging to anything, or colors such as stones have but that in fact colored nothing.

On this view, what we call "individual things" are ripples on the sea of a unified divine reality. The existence of each *just in itself* would be like that of a grin without a grinning face.

It is not being said that the existential unity of our universe with all its billions of galaxies is something obvious. Nevertheless, it is often claimed, some at least of its elements have such unity in rather an obvious way. This much, it is held, can be known by experimental physicists, or by all of us simply through considering our own conscious states. It can seem, too, that unless such unity were found in conscious states they would have no intrinsic value. A computer of the future might be able to reason with tremendous intelligence, far outclassing all humans. Its thoughts (assuming, and why not?, that they deserved this name) might be characterized by immense complexities. But if the complexities lacked unity-of-existence of the specially evident kind that is found in human consciousness, those thoughts would have no value in themselves. Their existence could not be self-justifying.

In looking at all this, a first point to notice is rather an abstract one. Our universe surely cannot be a collection of entities each with no spread in time or in space. How could anything lasting for no time at all be any different from nothing? Or how could any physical entity be real, had it absolutely no size? But when, instead of infinitely small whatnots which exist for no periods whatever, we have *entities extended in their existence*, why fancy that any such entity must have *precisely the same features* at all the spatiotemporal points over which its existence extends? Why could not the features differ from point to point, as Spinoza envisaged when he held that the entire cosmos was existentially unified divine thinking? F. H. Bradley described "a union of sameness and diversity" in which elements that were spread out, often very different from one another, still managed to be all of them aspects of a single existent. Why not something on those lines?

Bertrand Russell thought he could say why not. Abandoning the Spinozistic doctrines of Hegel and Bradley and of his own early years, Russell came to think as follows. An existentially unified whole might conceivably contain elements standing in "symmetrical" relationships such as *being a relative of*, or *being similar to*, or *being very near to*. (If Jack is in close proximity to Jill, then Jill is in close proximity to Jack.) In contrast, it could never contain elements standing in ones like *being the father of*, or *being smaller than*, or *being more dominant than*, all of which are "asymmetrical" – for if, e.g., I'm your father, then you aren't mine. An existentially unified reality could never contain asymmetries, Russell reasoned.

He is fairly clearly wrong, however. Take the case of the color orange. It has a red element and a yellow element. These are not two things existing separately from each other, yet why cannot the yellow element be *more dominant than* the red? Some shades of orange are much more strongly yellow than red, aren't they?

Existential Unities in Quantum Physics

Quantum physicists often maintain that various parts of our universe are united in their existence. Take a box containing two photons ("particles of light") that happen to be in the same quantum state (never mind what this means). How likely are they to be in different halves of the box? Suppose the existence of each photon is truly separate from that of the other. The possibilities are then: (*i*) photon number 1 to the left and photon number 2 to the right; (*ii*) photon number 2 to the left and photon number 1 to the right; (*iii*) both photons to the left; and (*iv*) both to the right. The probability that the photons are in different halves is therefore ONE-HALF. However, experiments show that it is actually ONE-THIRD. The strange fact is that cases (*i*) and (*ii*) are utterly identical, rather than just being indistinguishable by humans. The two photons are an existentially unified reality that appears in two locations.

If you think this impossible, then why? I refuse to believe that any saint has ever been seen in two places at once, yet tales on those lines are not quite so easily rejected as stories about bachelors observed to have two wives. Also it isn't just what pantheists say – it is instead very standard theology – that God is present in all locations simultaneously.

The physicists can point to many similarly suggestive cases. These, for instance:

(A) Superfluidity and superconductivity involve particles that move in large groups. It may still make sense to ask how many particles there are in each group, yet each particle can no longer be considered an independently real thing. Friction and electrical resistance would act on independently real particles, but here they are abolished. In SQUIDS, superconducting quantum interference devices, huge numbers of electrons can suddenly all "tunnel" through an obstacle as if they formed a single entity. In some good enough sense they do indeed form one.

(B) In experiments suggested by J. S. Bell, pairs of particles originating at the same point are found to have a very marked degree of "entanglement." Their behaviors, that is to say, remain strongly correlated no matter how far apart they move. Suppose the particles are photons. One of a pair hits a polarizer oriented in a direction chosen randomly by the experimenter, and gets through. Its perhaps far distant partner will then get through a similarly oriented polarizer without fail – although when photons all polarized identically are sent to a polarizer oriented at roughly 45 degrees to their direction of polarization, only about half get through.

Here the fact that the experimenter can select just any orientation shows that the photons of each pair cannot, before moving apart, somehow have reached agreement on how they were going to behave. Again, the orientation can be picked immediately before the photons hit the polarizers, meaning that not even messages moving at the speed of light could bring about such agreement. Suddenly facing the same choice of how to behave, the photons choose in the same way even when many kilometers apart. They behave as a single agent, not two independent realities. Now, similar entanglement is found in many other places. In fact, some degree of it is produced whenever two microscopic particles interact. From that point in time onwards, Paul Davies's *Other Worlds* insists, those particles "can no longer be considered as independently real things." When they subsequently interact with further particles, this only adds complications to their linkage instead of ending it. As Lee Smolin remarks in *The Life of the Cosmos*, "given any one electron, its properties are entangled with those of every particle it has interacted with, from the moment of its creation."

It follows that at least a large proportion of the atoms visible to our telescopes, and perhaps all of them, cannot be real independently of one another. We are driven to this conclusion whether or not we think, pantheistically, that individual things are mere aspects of God's reality.

(C) Quantum theory tells us that every particle has wave-like characteristics. All waves, in turn, have particle-like characteristics. We are dealing with realities which develop as waves that often spread out widely, but which then give rise to interactions at particular points which seem chosen at random. In *The Nature of the Physical World*, Arthur Eddington asks us to picture "the light waves that are the result of a single emission of a single atom on the star Sirius." When the wave-front reaches Earth, its energy "would seem to be dissipated beyond recovery over a sphere of 50 billion miles' radius." In fact, however, all the energy can concentrate itself into somebody's eye – it thereby becoming immediately certain that it cannot appear anywhere else, despite there being no faster-than-light messages saying (as Eddington puts it) "We have found an eye. Let's all crowd into it." So is talk of the expanding wave-front just a colorful way of expressing human ignorance of where a tiny particle was heading? Not so, Eddington replies. Phenomena of wave-interference rule out that interpretation. We must instead accept that a unified reality extended over the entire surface of the gigantic sphere, having at every point "a uniform chance of doing work."

Quantum Computers

The double-slit experiment illustrates the sort of wave-interference Eddington has in mind. Electrons are fired at a slit in a screen. Placed beyond the screen to catch them, a photographic plate becomes peppered as if by machine-gun bullets coming through a slit in a wall. But what happens when a second slit is made in the screen? Light and dark bands appear on the plate, suggestive of waves that have interacted after passing through the slits. The bands, though, are composed of dots where individual electrons have landed. Furthermore they are formed even when the electron source is so weak that no two electrons are in flight at the same moment.

Here people sometimes speak of "interacting possibilities." During the flight of any one electron, they say, "waves of possibilities" pass through the slits, subsequently interacting complexly so as to give the electron intricately varied chances of appearing at various places. However, *possibilities that interact complexly* raise a vigorous suspicion that they are actually existent realities as well. (Remember, you're a possibility yourself, but you aren't "a mere possibility." You are somebody actual as well as somebody possible.) Now, as David Deutsch argues in *The Fabric of Reality*, the suspicion would be all the more vigorous if the complex interactions solved very difficult problems, as he expects will soon occur inside what are called "quantum computers." Here "superposed" possibilities perform the computations. The more complicated the computations, the less plausible the view that they are carried out by possibilities that are "mere."

Being superposed is what is crucial here. Quantum computers operate with elements, sometimes as simple as single electrons, that are in combinations ("superpositions") of possible states which were viewed as strict alternatives by classical physics – physics before the discovery of the quantum world. Thanks to this, vastly many computations might some day be performed in parallel by elements that could handle hardly any of them if classical physics were right. A quantum bit or "qubit" is the information present when two possible states of a system are superposed. Two-qubit systems have performed 4 elementary computations simultaneously. A 32-qubit system might perform 2^{32} of them, which is over 4 billion. A 35-qubit system might perform 8 times as many again, and so forth. Here could be a means of cracking military codes by finding which gigantic prime numbers had been multiplied to generate numbers still more gigantic. A quantum computer might consider all the possibilities simultaneously. Again, truly intelligent machines might need to search vast databases at great speed. A quantum computer might examine every single entry at once.

So far, experimenters have constructed nothing beyond 10-qubit computers. The resulting computing power is trivial. The difficulty is that interactions with the environment tend to produce "decoherence," destruction of superposition, before calculations can be performed. The greater the number of qubits, the worse this problem becomes. But considerable progress could soon be made on one or other of many fronts. For instance, information might be passed from particle to particle before decoherence could dissipate it, this being precisely the kind of trick that evolution may actually have built into the workings of the human brain. Besides, quantum computing has taken place at temperatures which on standard arguments would seem much too high. Alexei Kitaev sees this as showing that some physical systems use a natural form of "quantum error correction," changes due to decoherence being reversed without first needing to be "read" or "measured" in a manner which would itself cause still more decoherence. Might that be another phenomenon the brain could exploit?

In effect, quantum computing could be of interest more than just as something supporting Deutsch's point that hugely complex developments in the quantum world cannot concern *mere possibilities*. True, this point might add to the charms of pantheism. It might help show that, even when of vast complexity, matters of actual existence need not involve a great many things each existing independently of the others. Quantum systems have a wholeness incompatible with such fragmentation. For our purposes, though, an equally major point is this. The kind of existential unity that Descartes famously attributed to the human mind, and which Spinoza then described as something possessed by a divine mind that includes all the things of our universe, could thrust itself on our attention in the place where Descartes found it. It could exist there if our minds are our brains, or parts or aspects of them, and if brain regions act as quantum computers.

Might Quantum Computing Occur Inside Brains?

Descartes writes in his *Sixth Meditation* that his mind is very different from his body because in it he can find "no parts." It is a complex realm of sensations, emotions, thoughts, acts of will, yet not of "parts" in the philosophically traditional sense. It contains no things separate from one another in their existence. Few philosophers of his day would have disagreed. Plato had insisted in his *Phaedo* that the soul of a human isn't just "a harmony," a smooth interaction of elements which might go their separate ways after that human's body had died.

Later writers have had similar convictions. (*a*) Locke's *Essay concerning Human Understanding* declares that wisdom and knowledge cannot exist in mere "juxtaposition of parts," a notion "than which nothing can be more absurd." (*b*) Leibniz, in his *Monadology*, imagines entering "as if into a mill" some gigantic machine alleged to have true consciousness. Finding there nothing but "parts which push one another," he concludes that these aren't in fact "anything which could explain a perception." That the parts interact by mere pushes is not what bothers him. Were they interacting magnetically, his reaction would be the same. Entities separate in their existence cannot form a conscious whole, no matter how they interact. (*c*) In *The Principles of Psychology* William James insists that "however complex the object may be, the thought of it is one undivided state of consciousness." (*d*) In the thirty-first of his *Collected Essays* Bradley dismisses as "really monstrous" any suggestion that the unity found in human consciousness consists in "no more than some relation or relations" between separately existing elements: relations of causal integration, perhaps, or of closeness in space or in time. (*e*) C. D. Broad, in *The Mind and its Place in Nature*, doubts whether elements genuinely separate in their existence could ever be regarded by anybody "except a philosopher engaged in philosophizing" as all that introspection reveals to us. The relationship of your mind to your toothache couldn't be on a par with that "of the British Army to Private John Smith." (*f*) *Problems from Locke*, by J. L. Mackie, points to "experiential content" as something we should hesitate to ascribe to computers, no matter how sophisticated their performance, since "the basic fact of occurrent awareness seems not to be analyzable into any simpler components."

How, though, can any of this make sense, granted that we lack immaterial souls? Scientists and philosophers of science perhaps provide the answer. (*i*) In their *The Undivided Universe*, David Bohm and Basil Hiley write that the elements of conscious states "flow into and out of" one another, evidence of "a basic similarity between the quantum behavior of a system of electrons for example and the behavior of mind"; "a rudimentary mind-like quality" is found "even at the level of particle physics." (*ii*) In "The Reality of the Quantum World" Abner Shimony suggests that without entities such as quantum theory describes, entangled in their very being, we could never make sense of "the holistic character of mind that our high-level experience reveals." (*iii*) In *Theories of Consciousness* William Seager, considering "the combination problem" of how the elements of a complex conscious state are united, asks us to remember that "a *quantum* whole is not simply the sum of its parts." (*iv*) Roger Penrose's *The Emperor's New Mind*, speaking of how normal consciousness is characterized by "its 'oneness' – as opposed to a great many independent activities going on at once," looks to quantum theory for an explanation. (*v*) Michael Lockwood's *Mind, Brain and the Quantum* is a sustained, philosophically expert defense of the same approach.

It would be wrong to seek quantum effects that unified all of one's mental processes into a whole whose every element was grasped with complete clarity. Descartes believed he was aware of something on those lines, but almost everyone now thinks him mistaken. The wholeness found in quantum systems is seldom a straightforward affair, however. Quantum entanglement may fuse all the galaxies seen by our telescopes into a system whose elements do not exist independently, yet nobody would call it a whole unified in any immediately evident way. It would be built up from innumerable subsystems each containing elements that were unified much more obviously because here the entanglement was much more marked, or because of other quantum phenomena, for instance of superposition. Now, the same would apply to any quantum unification present inside human brains. Lockwood writes that introspection, instead of revealing total mental unity, shows "degrees of co-consciousness," "overlapping," "a spectrum of degrees of connectedness."

The question, then, is not whether quantum theory could rescue the uncompromisingly simple views of Descartes. Instead we have to ask how quantum effects could generate unity of any sort that ordinary causal linkages couldn't. If brain regions act as quantum computers of a kind – if they make use of the existential overlaps, the failures to be real independently, which quantum physicists have identified – then just which quantum phenomena could be exploited here? In his various writings Penrose makes several suggestions. Maybe, he says, the "oneness" or "globality" found in conscious states is brought about as follows. Granted that possibilities viewed by classical physics as firm alternatives can in fact exist in quantum superposition, "*a single quantum state* could in principle consist of a large number of activities, all occurring simultaneously." Or perhaps a crucial role is played by "quantum correlations" of various types. Thus, there might be "large-scale quantum coherence" as suggested by Herbert Fröhlich, the coherence of "Bose–Einstein condensates." Some speak of "Bose–Einstein condensation" only when atoms (up to hundreds of millions of them) lose their individualities through cooling to near absolute zero, but Penrose uses the term whenever particles overlap markedly thanks to their wave-like natures. They may do so through having energy supplied to them so that they vibrate coherently – in a laser beam, for example, and perhaps also in the brain. There could therefore be cerebral holograms something like the holograms generated by lasers, Penrose thinks. In a hologram each part carries information about the whole.

Similar suggestions appear in the writings of Ian Marshall, Danah Zohar, and Stuart Hameroff. Yet aren't they on the wrong track, for wouldn't quantum coherence be lost very rapidly inside the brain? Perhaps not necessarily. Hameroff draws attention to microtubules, extremely tiny tubes inside nerve cells. These, Penrose writes, "might be able to isolate what is going on in their interiors from the random activity of the environment." Quantum entanglements could produce coherent activity in "microtubules collectively right across large areas," this then persisting "for something of the order of nearly a second."

Even far briefer periods could allow for impressively much quantum computing. Take a system encoding a few tens of qubits, maintain its coherence for a millisecond, and you'd be well on your way to founding a multitrillion-dollar industry.

The "What-it's-like" of Having Complex Consciousness

Imagine an ordinary computer – one making no use of quantum whole-ness – many trillion times more powerful than any in existence today. It might compose fine poetry, discuss philosophical questions brilliantly, or (when connected to a TV camera) judge the quality of a painting as expertly as anyone. Yet would there be, in the phrase originated by Timothy Sprigge, *anything which it was like to be* the computer? Would being the computer *feel like* anything?

In *Minds, Brains and Science* and in *The Mystery of Consciousness*, John Searle introduces two variants on Leibniz's mill. One is a computer built of old beer cans and powered by the breeze. Anything an ordinary computer of today could do, the beer cans computer could do better if made large enough, programmed well enough, and given time enough for its computations. Evaluate a painting? No problem! Produce books of philosophical psychology? Sooner or later, the beer can movements would generate them. But would building the computer be a case of creating a genuine mind? This could be a tedious issue of how you care to use the word "mind." The interesting point is that the computer would have no consciousness of a sort worth having for its own sake.

Admittedly my theory is that the beer cans, plus any rods, ropes, pulleys, or cogwheels linking them, would all be only elements of what I call a divine mind. This makes me a defender of panpsychism of a sort. But (as emphasized by Thomas Nagel in *Mortal Questions*) panpsychism of that sort, the view that the stuff of the universe has mental properties, is not panpsychism in the more familiar sense according to which trees and flowers, perhaps even rocks, have consciousness of a kind. A tree's parts wouldn't be clearly enough united to form a whole that had a consciousness intrinsically worth having, and neither would the parts of any beer cans computer, regardless of whether it was "conscious" in the sense of being able to evaluate paintings. What would being the computer feel like? It would not feel like anything.

Searle also imagines a room occupied by a man manipulating symbols in accordance with a complicated rule-book. The result of the man's labors is that questions in Chinese are answered expertly in that language, of which the man himself understands not a word. Considered as a whole, do the contents of the room know how to speak Chinese?

It might be tempting to say so. But the crucial point is that there would be no understanding of Chinese that was worth having for its own sake, instead of, say, for the sake of providing answers that justified the man's salary.

Imagine, again, trillions of individuals passing to one another slips of paper that bear the numbers zero or one. Each individual obeys very simple rules such as "Pass a zero to the person to your right whenever you are handed two zeros." In principle such a system could do far more than today's largest computers: compose superb poetry, perhaps. Could it feel like anything to be that system? Could there be anything intrinsically worthwhile in being it? Presumably not. Regardless of whether pantheism is correct, the system's parts would not be clearly enough united in their existence.

Unfortunately, talk of "being clearly enough united" can itself seem rather unclear. Let us therefore move on from considering the thousands of elements in one's awareness of a painting, the how-it-feels of experiencing all those elements *together*. Let us look at something else instead. How does it feel to experience areas of the painting as colored in various ways? This concerns what philosophers call "qualia."

Qualia

Qualia are phenomenal qualities: features of experiences such as just how it feels to be tickled, smell a rose, hear a musical note or see a color. Attached to a TV camera, a computer of today could distinguish between states inside it that corresponded to cakes with pink icing on the one hand, ones with yellow icing on the other. But while it could then sort the cakes by color, it could never experience pink and yellow as humans do.

Why not? It is because all a computer of today could ever know about its internal states would be *their structures*. Any complex computer must keep track of its activity-patterns. It can be commanded to report on them, then engaging in introspection of a kind. But it is computational structures that ordinary computers of today keep track of and introspect: structures that would be exactly the same if the computers, instead of operating through interactions of electrons, employed cogwheels, rods, and beer cans. Our knowledge of experienced colors, in contrast, is knowledge about the stuff from which various mental structures are built: knowledge of its qualitative nature.

Physicists, as Lockwood notes, though they describe the world's spatiotemporal structure in great detail, never say "how the structure is qualitatively fleshed out." Yet the world cannot be nothing but structure, structure, structure, no matter how far down we dive into its microscopic details! Without qualitative distinctions to make what's present at one point different from what's present at another, there could be no structure at all. Now, says Lockwood, when we experience qualia the intrinsic, qualitative nature of the world, or at least of part of it, "makes itself manifest" – a main message, he suggests, of Russell's *The Analysis of Matter*. It could not make itself manifest in the experiences (if they merit that name) of the cake-sorting computer.

It would not be graspable by that computer, no matter how much knowledge of physics had been fed into it. The computer might describe its parts in immense detail, aided by instruments with which it peered into itself, yet a grasp of anything more than structure would be for ever beyond it. Consider a man blind from birth onwards. No long telephone call from a physicist could give him knowledge of just how people feel when experiencing yellowness. And no ordinary computer could possess such knowledge, expert though it was at sorting colored objects.

Why might things be different in the case of the brain? Lockwood answers that various brain regions act as quantum computers. States in those regions can have a quantum wholeness that lets them know their own qualitative natures. Precisely how? We cannot yet tell. Quantum theory is only poorly understood. We have little idea of what kinds of quantum wholeness the brain is exploiting. The right language for discussing this area perhaps remains to be invented.

We can say at least this, nonetheless. Quantum computing in the brain would involve elements with partially fused identities. (Remember the two photons in the box.) A complicated cerebral reality, a brain state or a series of brain states, might therefore possess self-knowledge that was not rigidly restricted to what ordinary computers can possess. Knowing its own states, an ordinary computer could know nothing but various intricate patterns. It would have absolutely no way of gaining knowledge that was not just knowledge of structure. But what if states in the human brain can have quantum wholeness? In this case their self-knowledge might not be restricted in the same rigid fashion.

Many a philosopher looks on qualia as essential to intrinsic value. I cannot myself see why. To judge from their writings, the conscious states of various other philosophers have no qualia whatever. Mayn't they be good enough conscious states all the same? For a conscious state to be intrinsically worthwhile, all that is very plainly essential is its having a unity beyond mere structural unity. Its existence must not be comparable to that of a whirlpool or an ant colony. Qualia, however, can prove something to those of us acquainted with them. They establish that at least some conscious states *aren't* with an existence only of the whirlpool and ant-colony type.

Summing Up

Where is the relevance of all this to pantheism? Well, suppose we agree that groups of photons or electrons show signs of existential unification: the kind of unification, remember, that many philosophers view as characterizing minds and nothing else. Might this not do a little towards persuading us that our universe exists inside a divine mind? Again, suppose we indeed find such unification in our conscious states. Couldn't this nudge us a bit nearer to the same conclusion?

One thing that psychologists have learned, though, and that quantum physicists could have told them to look out for, is that any unification between elements of conscious states is not always entirely obvious. Descartes was mistaken on this point. The Cartesian picture of the mind's unity is far too simple. With respect to its obviousness, quantum unification comes in degrees, and the same is true of mental unification whether or not quantum effects play a part in it.

No pantheist need quarrel with any of this. Pantheists always have accepted that the elements of our universe are not mashed together indistinguishably. If you and I are aspects of one and the same divine reality, this still does not make me automatically aware of everything you think. Pantheism's cosmos is not (to borrow words from William James) "a large seaside boarding-house with no private bed-room in which I might take refuge from the society of the place." Bradley wrote that ultimate reality was "a single Experience," but he never meant anything on those lines. His pantheism was no denial of the world as we actually find it.

Bradley cannot have been entirely right, however, if a Platonic creation story is correct, for ultimate reality will in that case consist of more than *just a single* infinite mind. There will be infinitely many of them, for this is best. We inhabit a universe among countless others which exist inside one such mind. Contemplating everything worth contemplating, it is a mind of the finest possible type. The ethical need for it is immensely strong. Nonetheless, further minds of the same sort are needed as well.

Further Reading

The Bibliography is a guide to the works of many recent writers mentioned in this chapter. More details are given in my *Infinite Minds* and in Redhead's *From Physics to Metaphysics*, which emphasizes how quantum physicists so often find themselves forced to deny that systems "possess their own local properties independently of the holistic context." Shimony's "modified Whiteheadianism" (see Shimony's "On Mentality" and Whitehead's *Process and Reality*) is particularly intriguing: Penrose writes that something very similar must have been at the back of his own thoughts. Whitehead's extraordinary terminology could foreshadow a language we shall have to invent if we are to get a good grip on existential unity in quantum physics and elsewhere. The same perhaps applies to Bradley's strange terminology, or Hegel's.

Chapter 4

IMMORTALITY

Change in a Pantheistic Scheme of Things

Aristotle's *Metaphysics* remarks that any change in a divine being would be change for the worse. Spinoza sees things similarly. God, he writes in his *Short Treatise*, "cannot change into anything better" and must therefore be "immutable." But then, how can he or any other pantheist accept the obvious truth that ours is a world constantly varying? Chapter 1 sketched how the difficulty might be overcome. Any absolute alterations to a divine mind – meaning that first it was *in its entirety* something with one set of qualities, while subsequently it had another set – could only be for the worse, but in fact no alterations are ever absolute. Our world has a four-dimensional existence, as Einstein thought. The changes we experience are simply differences between successive cross-sections of the four-dimensional whole. This whole never itself alters.

On such a theory, although yesterday and tomorrow aren't parts of what we of today call "the world of today," this fails to make them non-existent. Suppose some man insists that they at least aren't in existence *now*. He ought to mean only that they aren't included in what's *now* relative to his utterance of the word "now," which merely says they don't inhabit the same cross-section of reality as the utterance in question.

In nontechnical language it can be hard to make this point. It can seem that Einstein, trying to comfort the relatives of his dead friend Michele Besso by explaining that common ways of thought were wrong about the status of past events, might just as well have talked of spherical cubes and wifeless husbands. Besso's life had not been annihilated absolutely, Einstein considered. It was *in existence back there* along the fourth dimension. But, the protest comes, doesn't saying a life "hasn't been annihilated" mean it is still being lived today? And mustn't this mean, *not* that it's today true that it's being lived "back there inside other cross-sections," but rather that it's lived in the situation of today, which isn't a cross-section of anything? Everything *at present* in existence is everything in existence, isn't it?

Well, ordinary thought does treat the dead as annihilated absolutely rather than only relatively. Folk typically pity or envy dead people in ways in which they wouldn't if convinced of their existence "back there." No matter how long and happy their lives were, the dead are pitied "because for them it's all finished," or no matter how miserable they used to be, they are envied because their sufferings "are now over." This is mirrored by ordinary language, tending to make it utter nonsense to talk of the dead as *in existence*. The important point, however, is that the situation as pictured by Einstein plainly isn't self-contradictory.

Suppose for argument's sake that ours is a universe where time "flows" as pictured by most people. The present constantly preys upon the past for the "stuff" of existence, taking this stuff and molding it into new shapes. Real existence is thus never anything but *existence now*. It has three dimensions and not four, we are supposing. The future isn't real yet, the past isn't real still. But what if a demon creates *another* universe in which the successive patterns of our universe are reproduced as patterns succeeding one another along a dimension of a four-dimensional reality, its parts all existing together? The demon-created universe is our universe as Einstein sees it, a universe in which Michele Besso's non-existence is never more than non-existence inside particular cross-sections. And how could we possibly know that our universe differed from Einstein's?

No Experiences Can Disprove Four-Dimensional Existence

Situations certainly develop in time. According to Einstein, though, they develop in a manner interestingly like that in which a pattern of interwoven threads develops along the length of a carpet. The dead and the as-yet-unborn are not alive today. However, the difference between living today and living in a distant century may be not too dissimilar from the difference between living on Earth and living in some remote galaxy. Now-ness can be as relative as here-ness. (What's "here" to me can be "over there" to you.) The world, Einstein wrote, has a four-dimensional structure, and experiments never find in this structure "any sections which represent 'now' objectively" – in any fashion, in other words, to which the experiments point. This, he continued, need not make us dismiss "happening and becoming" as useless concepts. Still, it renders it "natural to think of physical reality as a four-dimensional existence instead of, as hitherto, the evolution of a three-dimensional existence" (*Relativity: The Special and the General Theory*, 15th edition, Appendix 5).

What Einstein recognized is that observers moving relative to one another will find it simplifies their calculations if they differ in how they draw their "now-lines": lines connecting events all counted as "happening simultaneously," lines that divide spacetime into successive segments. No experiments could demonstrate that one way of drawing the lines was right and all the others wrong. As James Jeans remarked in *The Mysterious Universe*, things moving relative to one another treat any absolute distinction between space and time with as little respect as cricket balls give to the distinction between a cricket field's length and its breadth.

This doesn't mean that such an absolute distinction must be fictitious. After all, *a second, "anti-Einsteinian" demon* could take a four-dimensional model of the world's history and cut it into three-dimensional slices. These, the second demon could claim, corresponded to situations each in turn created while the preceding situation was annihilated. Now, suppose physicists tried to refute this. Whatever evidence they brought forward would be evidence of what the world's patterns were; yet couldn't those patterns appear in our second demon's slices just as easily as side by side in a four-dimensional whole? Consider Richard Feynman's point that calculations are simplified if the positrons entering into various reactions are treated as electrons moving backwards in time for brief periods, prior to again moving forwards. To anyone familiar with the Einsteinian approach, such *temporal zigzagging* could look far neater than the alternative, which is that each electron helps conjure into existence a further electron plus a positron, next fusing suicidally with the positron while the newly born electron continues onwards through time. But can this firmly prove that the zigzagging is real? The second demon would laugh at so quaint a suggestion.

Equally, however, our first, "Einsteinian" demon would laugh at the idea that anything in successive three-dimensional situations could prove they *weren't* mere cross-sections of a greater whole. This point applies to patterns of personal experience quite as much as to laboratory evidence. The exhilaration of fast running, fear of the unknown future, relief at inability to remember even which toe had been aching, could all of them exist inside a four-dimensional reality.

But why, if the world exists four-dimensionally, do we experience it as developing *from* the past *towards* the future? A standard reply runs as follows. Near the Big-Bang extremity of its four-dimensional existence, our universe possesses great thermodynamic orderliness. Events successively more removed from the Bang almost always possess less and less of it. Living systems, however, are like backward-moving eddies in a stream. They exploit the general flow towards thermodynamic disorder so as to increase their own order. In brains, this permits controlled transfer of information from points closer to the Bang to points farther away from it, which is why we "remember the past instead of the future."

For our purposes it hardly matters whether this standard reply is correct. What's crucial is only that, like the rest of the world, the realm of conscious experience runs not by magic but by physical laws: laws that specify correlations between the pattern of events at any one moment and the patterns at other moments. Now, exactly the same correlations can be present whether or not the world exists in a four-dimensional way.

Let us hope, though, that it does exist in such a way. For one thing, this would allow our thoughts to be real in more than the piecemeal fashion in which a train's progress across a continent is real. Any thought that is at all complex does not merely take time to generate. Instead, the thought is itself something spread out over time. But now, what if past and future situations do not actually exist? What if they have nothing more than *was-existence* and *will-be-existence*? In this case the elements of a complex thought are real only one after another. The thought as a whole is never actually there, much as a train is never actually at two railway stations.

On the Einsteinian picture, in contrast, such thoughts truly can be there in their entirety. They can even have wholeness of the kind considered in the previous chapter, a unity of existence where parts are abstractions only. And while there may be no firm proofs in this area, Michael Lockwood seems right in saying that the reality of our thoughts and experiences is not simply piecemeal, a case of "first this bit exists, and then it doesn't but the next one does, etcetera." When musical notes arrive in swift succession we seem to experience several of them together. As Lockwood points out, this supports both Einstein's worldview and the idea that quantum computing occurs in our brains. In the realm of the quantum, the parts of various wholes are not fully separate in their existence.

Immortality of a First, Einsteinian Type

Einstein may never have used the term "immortality" in this connection, yet in his world we could all be considered immortal in an interesting sense. Time no longer has to be regarded as "the flood on which the oldster wakes in the night to shudder at its swollen black torrent cascading him into the abyss" (D. C. Williams). Einstein and Besso will never have undergone absolute annihilation.

One way of viewing the matter could be this. Extending along a time dimension of a reality that exists four-dimensionally, humans may not be immortal in the sense that their earthly careers stretch indefinitely far beyond their births; however the four-dimensional reality, humans included, exists forever in time of another sort. The passage of this other kind of time, time in a somewhat different sense of the word "time," is not an affair of passing seconds, days, centuries. Instead it consists in the fact that alterations *could in principle be occurring* although they never in fact occur.

They could in principle be occurring because there would be no contradiction in the entire four-dimensional situation changing. It could in principle be replaced by a series of other four-dimensional situations, each noticeably different from its predecessor. It could even be replaced by total emptiness. Lack of all actual changes of this type would not mean that they were ruled out logically – that they couldn't conceivably be occurring. Well, the time in which they could conceivably be occurring is a time in which you and I can exist eternally, if our world is a four-dimensional whole that never in fact alters.

There is a tie between this way of thinking and very ordinary ways of thought. Imagine a world divided into two regions, each experiencing a freeze at intervals. When frozen, a region does not change at all. The first region undergoes alterations for 3 years, then remains frozen for a year, then starts altering again for another 3 years, and so forth. The second region goes through a similar cycle, but here each set of alterations takes 5 years instead of 3. Every so often, therefore, both regions must be frozen together for a period. During that period, time passes in the two-regioned world although nothing changes in it. There is no logical absurdity here, and nothing which clashes with common ways of thinking. What is more, no clash seems caused even by saying that outside the two regions there exists nothing whatever. Yet if nothing existed apart from them, reality as a whole would sometimes progress through time without the least change.

Immortality of a Second Type: An Afterlife

Spinoza denies life after death. He does sometimes call us immortal, but probably the only good sense to be found in his words is as follows. The pantheistic cosmos which he calls "God or Nature" exists eternally in the sense just now examined – it is, as we'd say today, a four-dimensional reality that is never replaced by anything different – and therefore human minds (like all other things) are never wiped from existence in the absolute fashion that Einstein rejected. Nevertheless we shall have no experiences at dates beyond our burials, Spinoza tells us firmly.

Why ever not? May we not have a right to life after death? Even if our experiences are simply elements in a divine mind's thinking, why shouldn't we have new ones after our bodies had died? Suppose some scientist has created a fully conscious computer which enjoys its thought processes. The scientist has no right to smash it, simply because of having created it. And the position may strike us as no different when an immensely intelligent extraterrestrial has simulated that computer and its workings inside his, her or its own head through thinking about them in immense detail. Although a simulation, the new, in-the-head computer would truly perform computations. Its thoughts would truly be had by it, despite being mere subpatterns of the extraterrestrial's thinking. So, wouldn't it be morally ugly for the extraterrestrial to annihilate it through ceasing to think about it? If a computer outside a head can be happy, so can a computer inside the head.

Consider now the divine mind inside which we supposedly exist. Picture it as having thought all the way through some person's life up to the moment of bodily death. Why should not the life continue onwards, our world's physical laws ceasing to govern it? Those laws, after all, are supposedly a mere matter of how the divine mind thinks inside the tiny region of its thinking that is the universe familiar to us. Well, why would it not think *as well* about lives that continued outside the region? Wouldn't this be less ugly than thinking about lives that ended completely?

Human thoughts continuing after the deaths of human bodies would be miracles in a sense, but in a pantheistic picture the miracles, radically new ways in which events took place, would simply be cases where the divine thoughts took on a radically new character – and why not, if it were something good? No breaks in the normal course of things would disturb the region of the divine thinking which included the human bodies. This region, the world at present known to us, would be a realm whose laws of physics were never superseded. It would be completely miracle-free. Yet while John Brown's body decayed in the region in question, the thoughts of John Brown could continue elsewhere with much the same structures as before. Outside a pantheistic scheme of things this might be a ridiculous fantasy. Inside one, it ought quite to be expected.

Could we picture the structures of entire human bodies as continuing onwards in dimensions beyond those of the physical world, whereas in that world the bodies burned or rotted? Think of a strip running across a floor, then splitting into one branch that struggles on for a while before fading away, plus another that rises up above the floor. Peter van Inwagen has imagined something rather similar. "Perhaps," he has written, "at the moment of each man's death, God removes his corpse and replaces it with a simulacrum which is what burns or rots" (in Edwards, ed., *Immortality*). The corpse itself is then revived for an afterlife. But Robert Nozick may do rather better when he toys with the idea that at death "a person's organized energy" is what "bubbles out orthogonally" into new dimensions. What he'd consider essential, Nozick specifies, would be organization of the sort found in a computer program that captured the person's "intellectual mode" and "personality pattern."

In an afterlife I'd not expect to find my thoughts linked to anything like a human body. Nonetheless I might recognize the thoughts as *mine* because, for one thing, they continued (at least at first) along the lines I had grown used to. I'd hope, as well, to recognize dead friends by becoming aware of their thoughts, finding that they shared various of my memories. My personal identity, I suspect, depends as little on my ever *really having had* a body as it does on my toenails. What if my life up to date had been lived by an immaterial soul deceived by Descartes's very powerful demon into thinking it had a body? The life would have been mine all the same.

Afterlives, if we have them, might be much as pictured by many religious folk, both pantheists and nonpantheists. People surviving bodily death could come to share the wonders of divine thought, losing much of their individuality. Keith Ward expects us all to "pass, as most theists think, into the wider reality of God," perhaps even becoming "one reality with God" and "knowing God wholly"; we might share God's knowledge of "the whole history of the universe." Yet it could be hoped that such changes would take place only gradually – for mightn't suddenly knowing the whole history of the universe erode one's individuality quite as drastically as suddenly changing into a tadpole with its extremely limited thoughts?

Could we gain limitlessly wide-ranging knowledge even in the very long term, if matters are as pantheists believe? Wouldn't many items of knowledge exist only inside severely circumscribed regions of the divine thinking, for instance knowledge of exactly how it felt to be some particular human with all of that human's ignorance? Even if coming to know "the whole history of the universe," or "knowing God wholly," would we not remain unaware of quite how it had felt to be Mozart? Spinoza's idea of *a divine overview* could be helpful here. Only limited beings can know just how it feels to be limited. (How could you know precisely how it felt to be as ignorant as humans are, were your mind flooded with knowledge of everything worth knowing? How could you experience all of the typical human fear of death, viewed as absolute annihilation, if fully aware that nobody undergoes such annihilation?)

Still, the divine reality could have a center at which everything was appreciated in a single glance. Here the hopes and fears of individual humans could be known "as if telepathically." This would involve something fairly close to knowledge of just how being a human feels.

Suppose, that's to say, that telepathy did in fact work. You might then get a very good idea of what it is like to be Mr. Smith, thoroughly frightened, without yourself thinking your name "Smith" or being alarmed for your safety. You could even get a very painful appreciation of Mr. Smith's rheumatism. Now, recall that in his *Ethics* Spinoza distinguishes between God "insofar as he is considered as constituting the essence of the human mind" – which could best be taken as meaning those regions of the divine mind that *are* human minds in all their limitations – and God "insofar as he possesses the ideas of all things." The divine reality includes an overview of all its parts, a seeing of them all together, and one of its ingredients is what I call "as if telepathic" knowledge of how it feels to be limited, for instance through being human. In the later sections of his *Ethics* Spinoza seems to say that this element of the divine reality not only knows humans well but loves them, or at least their better aspects.

People thinking along pantheistic lines might prefer to use the word "God" not (as Spinoza does) to name the divine reality as a whole, but rather as a label for such a central, "overviewing" element. Again, they might want to call this element *a divine person*. Experiencing and interacting with the central element or person would be awesome.

"Knowing God wholly" would always remain infinitely beyond us, I suspect. Even so, we could gain a constantly increasing share of all that is worth knowing. This might often be very different from memorizing more and more volumes of some infinitely large encyclopedia. What it is like to sing, chat, watch sunsets, create works of art, ski, is part of what's worth knowing. Why think an afterlife would contain no new knowledge of things rather like these? It could be lived with friends from earthly times and with excitements on a par with those of skiing, even if no human bodies were involved.

What about friends who had long been dead, or people of much earlier centuries? Wouldn't it be impossible to interact with them in any ordinary way because, by the time you had died, wouldn't they have outclassed you (in their share of the divine knowledge or in their degree of fusion with a divine person) by as much as humans outclass frogs or insects? Not necessarily, granted that an Einsteinian view of time is right. All the dead could enter the time dimension of an afterlife as a single group, without the sad consequence that those dying in earlier centuries had *wasted their time* by lying unconscious in their graves while waiting for the others to join them.

Would truly awful people survive, or would their lives be simply not worth preserving? Would there be afterlives for dogs or dolphins? In an afterlife I'd hope to meet many a previous dog, though feeling surprised if coming across a former mass murderer.

Immortality, Type Three: The Continued Existence of Something that had Carried Our Life-Patterns

The cells of our bodies are like candle flames, their atoms constantly replaced by new ones. Only their structures live on. But how then can we be the same people from year to year? Some philosophers speak of Pure Egos that experience our changing mental states while themselves never in the least altering, yet this can look a flat contradiction. Others describe mental states as carried by immaterial souls which do alter, but not with constant renewal of material as in human bodies, flames, or rivers. The nowadays standard story, however, is that structural continuity – like that of a path winding through a wood – is what keeps us always the same individuals.

There may be difficulties with this standard story, though. For a start, would completely unbroken continuity be crucial? If you dropped out of existence, would it make sense to talk of *you* as coming back after a millisecond?

Next, imagine *a splitting into branches* of what had been you until then. The "transporters" of science fiction (such as *Star Trek*) sometimes malfunction with results of this type. Would each branch still be you?

Might repeated duplication, perhaps by some device that destroyed your body while recording its details so as to be able to recreate its structure, mean that a million people could all of them be you? (Assume that all the brain traces that allow you to remember things could be duplicated successfully.) And if so would you – before being duplicated – live in terror when told that the million would be tortured? Would you view this as equivalent to being tortured a million times?

My personal identity isn't, I trust, a matter only of structural continuity, whether or not completely unbroken. For if structural continuity were all that unified my successive mental states, wouldn't my mental life be too split up to have much intrinsic value? Would my thoughts have any reality that wasn't merely piecemeal like the reality of a train's progress from country to country? Could I ever experience an entire complicated idea or a sequence of musical notes *as a single whole*? People would answer these questions in very different ways. It would be pointless to repeat everything leading to my own answers. The thing to notice is instead this. Suppose there are no afterlives. Suppose also that Einstein was wrong about our world's four-dimensional existence, so that complex thoughts and experiences of musical sequences exist only in piecemeal fashion. Even so, I could draw comfort from the notion that all the things of our universe are mere aspects of a single existent somewhat as a lake's color and length are aspects of the lake. This could give me a personal identity which amounted to more than mere structural continuity. Might it not even give me immortality of a sort?

As the previous chapter noted, there are general grounds for thinking our universe more than a mere collection of entities each with no spread in space or in time. (How could any physical entity be real if without any size or if lasting for no time at all? And why fancy that any one entity stretching though space or time must have just the same characteristics at every single point over which its existence extends?) Furthermore, quantum physicists describe fairly clear signs of existential unity: when two photons in a box are in the same quantum state, for instance, or when the properties of various particles are markedly entangled. Also, examination of one's own consciousness can indicate that some regions, at least, of our universe carry highly complex patterns yet are unified in their existence. Now, all this can suggest that existential unification characterizes the universe in its entirety. In consequence, might not you and I have something worth treating as immortality of a third kind? It would lie in the continued presence of a single existent which, carrying our life-patterns until we died, would carry also those of all who lived after us. This single existent would be our universe or a divine mind in which this universe is contained.

The idea of personal identity is only fuzzily defined in ordinary thought and language. It thus makes little sense to insist that all who had wanted an indefinitely prolonged future *for themselves*, but who now disbelieved in an afterlife, would still have something to hope for: namely, that an existentially unified reality, something whose parts were mere aspects or abstractions, carried their life-patterns and would carry the patterns of other lives in future centuries. Many would deny that anything on these lines would be relevant *to them personally*. On their preferred definition of it, personal identity could never survive without sameness of personality: sameness of character. It might follow that you ought not to fear some painful injury to be inflicted on the body that now counted as *yours*, just so long as you knew your personality would beforehand be destroyed through brainwashing; for wouldn't the body that was injured then be that of *another person*?

Those favoring this approach could not be at fault linguistically, any more than if they demanded slightly more food than various other people in anything they would describe as "a breakfast" or allowed slightly less white into anything they'd call "dark gray."

When, that is to say, words are vague, individuals have a right to use them somewhat as they please. But note, now, that the persistence of *something existentially unified that had carried one's mental life* is what many have chosen to mean by "surviving bodily death." The immaterial soul was traditionally pictured as just such a unified entity, and doubt was often thrown on any need for it to be free of abrupt personality changes. (Entry into heaven, it was said, produced instant and radical improvements in character in all but the most saintly souls. Even on Earth, sudden repentances could involve great transformations.) Clearly, the continued presence of intelligent life for many further centuries wouldn't be sufficient, not even in an existentially unified cosmos, for survival *of one's personality* through all those centuries; but nonetheless, mightn't it provide for something worth the name of "personal survival"? Personal identity strikes me as a concept nebulous enough to allow us to answer Yes just as much as No.

Hindus in the tradition of the *Chandogya Upanishad* look forward to a "dissolving into Brahman" in which (they must surely think) their personal identities would not be wholly destroyed, else how could they look forward to it as they do? It isn't as a man in torment looks forward to annihilation. Their idea is that they will lose their individual personalities when fading into the heart of a pantheistic universe, yet that this will bring good to themselves.

Here is one way of approaching the affair. Suppose you became con-vinced that you and all other living creatures were simply elements in an existentially unified cosmic whole. You might then see aiding others, humans and animals alike, as producing *self-benefits* of an odd type. Whenever trying to benefit yourself, you could well conclude, what you had really wanted was benefit to something existentially unified that carried your ever-varying states of mind. You would now see this sort of benefit as produced whenever you helped another human or even a whale – for if our world's complexities are always mere aspects of a single existent, then all the world's conscious beings "are, at some level, one," as Derek Parfit expresses it; one and the same all-encompassing thing is living the lives of all. Well, benefits of that type could continue onwards indefinitely through the persistence of the stuff of which the cosmos was made, and through its continuing to carry the patterns of living intelligence.

Does the Third Kind of Immortality Remove
All Need for an Afterlife?

If we could look forward to the kind of immortality just now examined, would our chances of an afterlife be ruined? Would we have to look forward to immortality of that sort instead?

Suppose, that is, that after our bodies had died we really would be immortal in a sense, drawing benefits of a sort, through the continu-ance of something existentially unified (a divine mind, or at least an existentially unified cosmos) which carries our life-patterns at the present instant. Why hope for anything more than this? Would it not be enough by itself?

The right reaction, presumably, is that an afterlife and the continu-ance of the existentially unified something would be fully compatible, and that there would be reason enough to wish for both of them together. What if the life of your child, your spouse or your friend is merely an aspect of a divine mind, and the mind in question will exist forever? For bodily death to terminate the life could still be something ugly.

The three possible forms of immortality are entirely distinct, so that any one of them might be had while the other two were not. However, it looks as if we could well have all three conjointly.

The Chances of Immortality of One Kind or Another

Picture a world of severely limited, separately existing things that spring into being, then undergo absolute annihilation. Surely this would be far from what one would expect if ethical requirements had creative power. Once, therefore, we had accepted a Platonic creation story, we could seem forced to believe in immortality of the first and third kinds.

Those kinds, though, can be argued for even without Plato's assistance. (A) Philosophers such as J. M. E. McTaggart, J. J. C. Smart, and Adolf Grünbaum maintain that an "absolute" flow of time, a series of changes to reality in its entirety, cannot be described without contradiction. If they are right, there are logical grounds for the belief that lives are never wiped out absolutely. Other grounds for this belief come from the triumphs of Einsteinian relativity theory. (B) Similarly – see the previous chapter – fairly abstract reasoning on the one hand, various scientific discoveries on the other, can suggest that reality forms an existentially unified whole. If it does, then that whole is living your life in some parts of it, and mine in others. It will live other lives when ours have ended.

The case of immortality of the second kind, the afterlife, is altogether different. Here is an immortality that certainly cannot be expected just on abstract or logical grounds, and there can seem to be no evidence for it. Think of what scientists now know about how minds are related to brains. It could easily seem fantastic for mental life to continue onwards beyond bodily death, let alone outside the spacetime in which we find ourselves. An afterlife can look preposterous unless we accept something like the divine reality of conventional religious systems, or a Platonic creation story, or both. I think it has to be *both*. A divine reality – perhaps pantheism's infinitely complex realm that the dead could explore, or perhaps a divine person who could share with them the wonders that he contemplates – strikes me as too hard to swallow when existing for no reason whatever. In contrast, a divine reality that exists *because this is ethically required* can be accepted readily enough when once you have grown used to the idea. Against the background of such a reality, an afterlife can be plausible.

What items of evidence, then, could give plausibility to the Platonic creation story and therefore to the idea of an afterlife?

Let us begin by remembering that the world portrayed by modern science is apparently *not* a series of severely limited, separately existing things, each suffering absolute annihilation soon after it has sprung into being. It is a world which can plausibly be viewed as an infinitely complex, fully unified and eternally existing whole. It could well contain infinitely many gigantic domains each worth calling "a universe." It could be just the sort of thing that a Platonic creation story would lead us to expect.

There are three further main items of evidence, to be discussed in the next chapter. First, there is the sheer truth that a world exists. Second, the world's events are orderly in a fashion leading us to speak of *causal laws*. And third, those laws permit the existence of intelligent living beings. A Platonic creation story can make sense of all this.

Further Reading

The theory that the world exists four-dimensionally is argued for by Adolf Grünbaum, J. J. C. Smart, Timothy Sprigge, and D. C. Williams. In his superb "The Myth of Passage" Williams holds that death is less fearsome on this theory. Sprigge writes that our experiences "are all just eternally there." For the works of these writers and of others this chapter has mentioned, see the Bibliography.

Sidney Shoemaker's "Time without Change" discusses a world divided into regions each frozen at intervals, and sometimes frozen simultaneously for lengthy periods.

Peter van Inwagen's idea that God removes corpses so as to revive them, replacing them by simulacra, is one of many curious things in Edwards, ed., *Immortality*. Robert Nozick's "orthogonal bubbling out of organized energy" appears in the second chapter, "Dying", of *The Examined Life*.

Keith Ward's *Religion and Creation* contrasts the immortality theories of the Chandogya and Taittariya *Upanishads*. In the first we lose our individualities so quickly that we never really know we are dissolving into Brahman, whereas in the second we retain them while roaming the divine reality.

In *Self-Knowledge and Social Relations* John King-Farlow develops a language where the subject of everything is "It," an existentially unified cosmic whole. A cry for mother becomes "Let It be Mama'd here!" He gets close to saying that people who deliberately harm others show their ignorance of how they and these others are merely aspects of the same one existent.

My own struggles with such topics include "The Value of Time" in the *American Philosophical Quarterly* of April 1976.

Chapter 5

EXISTENCE, CAUSATION, AND LIFE

The World's Existence as an Item of Evidence

Seeking evidence in support of a Platonic creation story, and therefore of belief in such marvels as an afterlife, could we find some in the sheer fact that *there exists a world of things*, not just a Platonic realm of mere possibilities?

(*i*) Philosophers sometimes say that something or other simply had to exist, through logical necessity. Some have argued that a divine person is by definition perfect and therefore must exist because existence (or maybe *necessary existence*) is an element in perfection; but this is now very widely rejected. A few others, in particular David Lewis, have reasoned that absolutely everything that is logically possible exists somewhere. "Being actual rather than merely possible" ought then to mean something much like "existing here, not merely over there." A difficulty with this approach was raised in chapter 1, however. Among the things that are logically possible, things containing no contradiction, there are worlds that start off orderly and become disorderly. At any instant disorder could make its appearance in a world which had been orderly right up to that point. People could suddenly turn into pebbles, puddles or puffs of smoke. Now, the range of ways in which our world could become extremely disorderly is far greater than the range of ways in which it could continue to be orderly. Lewis's theory would thus seem to give us grounds for expecting to die at once – because of being about to become pebbles, fall to bits, vanish, or suffer any of countless other disasters.

(*ii*) Would "*You can't conceive anything without imagining somebody who observes it*" prove that there must always have existed one observer at least? Would it even be true? Most people do not think so. There looks to be no contradiction in the entire cosmos vanishing all of a sudden. Similarly, there is nothing absurd in the concept of never-ending emptiness, the eternal absence of all actual things. Logic shows only the idiocy of arguing that emptiness is what we actually have.

(*iii*) What if nothing had ever existed? Then, sure enough, there would have been nobody to be puzzled by anything. Yet why shouldn't we be puzzled by how puzzlement's prerequisites have been fulfilled? Suppose a bomb had exploded 6 feet away from you. Would "*You couldn't puzzle over anything if you'd been destroyed!*" reduce your surprise at finding yourself alive?

(*iv*) "But what's so surprising in the existence of the natural world? Isn't it something every bit as natural as you can get?" – "Naturalness" such as Nature has necessarily, in the way that bachelors have wifelessness, does strike some folk as grounds for refusing to ask why there is any such thing as Nature. There seems little hope of proving them wrong. But there seems no prospect, either, of showing that they must be right. Hume theorized that the universe had no explanation whatever. His idea was that we should be puzzled only by matters which conflict with past experience; and doesn't past experience indicate that there's a universe? Yet past experience surely never told Hume that the universe had no explanation. Further, he quickly came to see that we can learn nothing from experience all by itself. In order to show us more than "blooming, buzzing confusion" (as William James expressed it) the information coming from our senses has to be interpreted, and it cannot itself supply the principles needed for starting to interpret it. This is the message of Hume, of Kant and of contemporary philosophy of science. Now, "*Things have reasons for their existence*" can seem among the principles we need.

(*v*) Could the reason for the world's existence at any hour be that it had existed at the previous hour, and so on backwards forever? Might the Big Bang have been preceded by a Big Squeeze, and this in turn by another Big Bang, and so forth, in an infinity of cycles? Well, Leibniz pointed out that a geometry book's contents really aren't explained when you say it was copied from an earlier geometry book and so on *ad infinitum*. Similarly, it would not help if you said the book had existed for infinitely long. Some Muslims believe this about the Koran, yet they do not treat its existence as an ultimate brute fact and none of Allah's doing.

(*vi*) There has been much excitement over the idea that our universe has a total energy of zero or nearly zero. The gravitational energy holding it together should be counted as "negative energy," physicists maintain, and this energy could more or less exactly cancel all the positive energy tied up – remember $E = mc^2$ – in its enormously many tons of material. Mightn't it therefore have come to exist as *a quantum fluctuation* rather like the particles that are (thanks to the probabilistic nature of quantum physics) forever flickering into existence in empty space? Or again, some physicists say, could it not be that time was more and more space-like or more blurred, or spacetime more and more foamy, at ever earlier moments in the Big Bang, meaning there was no definite first instant of cosmic history at which things leapt into being?

The right reaction is that why there is any world, not just a Platonic realm of mere possibilities, could never be answered by describing the world as possessing qualities like that of obeying laws of quantum physics or of having a time dimension with such and such characteristics. The question would remain of why these qualities were had by anything real. What if we are told that the laws of quantum physics themselves assert that they will have actually existing things to govern *not certainly*, because quantum physics is only probabilistic, but *almost certainly* since some "quantum-fluctuational creation process" will be almost sure to operate? We can still ask whether that's indeed right, and if so, why. Consider a law saying that little green imps must almost certainly exist. It tells us there is almost surely something – some actual set of imps – to which it applies. But is it correct? And if it is, then for what reason?

(*vii*) Some theologians hold that God is simple through being infinite – their idea being that, for example, *knowing everything* is less complex than *knowing W and X while remaining ignorant of Y and Z*. Again, God is sometimes said to be Pure Being and therefore simple. God's semblance of having numerous qualities, such as *knowing all about cats*, is nonetheless "well-founded": *God knows all about cats* is "more nearly true" than *God doesn't*. Or finally, God's presence is viewed as a straightforward affair because God is not dependent (or *not even possibly* dependent) on any factor external to God. But even if some of this made sense, it could seem that it would have been much simpler if God had never existed. Besides which, saying God does not depend on any external factor isn't the same as declaring that God exists reasonlessly. The presence of a divine mind could be due to something not "outside" it in any straightforward fashion. The divine mind could exist thanks to its own ethical requiredness.

Evidence from the World's Causal Orderliness

Why does our world contain causal regularities? Why do magnets regularly attract iron? When our planet pulls people towards it, how can we explain this otherwise than by saying "It's because they're heavy," which can sound too much like identifying opium's "dormitive virtue" as the factor that puts you to sleep? How come, even, that nails move when hammers hit them? "Hammers are heavy as well" may not seem a sufficient reply.

Whenever wishing to explain one causal law, some people have claimed, you would have to point to another that was more fundamental. ("Why does water regularly become steam when splashed on white hot iron? It's because molecules in fast thermal motion regularly break free from one another.") If that were right, there would no doubt be some very most fundamental law or laws that had no explanation at all. Still, why on earth should we think it right? Is it at all plausible that, at some level or other, events present themselves in orderly patterns for absolutely no reason?

A. J. Ayer thought it plausible. He argued that "always being orderly" meant something like "always defying mere chance," and that getting events to obey the laws of chance was none too easy. For casinos to stay in business, he pointed out, roulette wheels must be engineered very accurately. "Doing better than chance" when guessing cards would have no tendency to prove that telepathy worked, he wrote. All that could be impressive would be doing better than most card-guessers do. Had everybody always guessed correctly, he would have seen no problem in it. It would be a regularity characterizing our world, and that would be that! But this strikes most people as showing the bankruptcy of Ayer's extreme "empiricism," an awful instance of his failure to follow Hume, Kant, and William James when they teach that we get nowhere when we rely just on the material that streams in from our senses, looking to this material itself for all the principles we could need in order to interpret it. Not as bad, no doubt, as Ayer's earlier idea that (as in George Orwell's *1984*!) truths about the past were truths only about so-called records and traces, but getting on for as bad.

Still, what possible alternative is there to declaring that events "just obey laws, and that's that"? Must we conclude that talk of opium's dormitive virtue is on something like the right track, saying that objects like hammers have an ultimately inexplicable ability, a "concussive virtue," to impart their motion to others such as nails? Or perhaps that a divine individual exerted totally inexplicable power when decreeing "Nails shall always move if hammers hit them" or when setting up the laws of dynamics that govern hammer–nail interactions? Would it be a brute fact – not merely beyond what humans can explain, but without any explanation at all – that when the divine being wanted things to happen, they regularly did happen?

I recommend taking a Platonic route instead. Why are the world's patterns orderly? Why, more particularly, do they have orderliness such as makes us speak of "laws of cause and effect"? It is because their orderliness is worth contemplating for a divine mind inside which they have their being. The divine mind itself exists because this is ethically required. Although the creative power of an ethical requirement would never be provable by logicians, we could have some degree of insight into it. Located in a Platonic realm of eternal realities, any ethical requirement for the existence of a divine mind would at least pass one crucial test. Unlike being at the North Pole, or blueness, or the fact that two 6s make 12, it would be something of which "creatively effective" could meaningfully be said. As candidates for creating this or that, *requirements for the existence of things* are realities in the right general category.

Evidence from Cosmic Fine-Tuning

Intelligent life comes from Darwinian selection, a process acting for billions of years on progressively more complex systems. But why was a suitable environment available for all those years? Why, even, were Nature's laws such as to permit the existence of intelligent living beings?

Such questions long seemed absurd to many people. They have aroused more interest recently, thanks to what is described as cosmic "fine-tuning." Slight changes to basic cosmic parameters would have made life's evolution impossible, it is now often held. Claims like the following have been made by numerous scientists:

(a) Alterations by less than one part in a billion to the expansion speed early in the Big Bang would have led to runaway expansion, everything quickly becoming so dilute that no stars could have formed, or else to gravitational collapse inside under a second.

(b) Life was able to evolve only because the universe at early instants had been immensely smooth instead of turbulent. As estimated by Roger Penrose, it had to be smooth to one part in one followed by a thousand trillion trillion trillion trillion trillion trillion trillion trillion trillion trillion zeros.

(c) Minimal tinkering with the strength of one of the forces controlling atomic nuclei, the nuclear weak force, would have destroyed the hydrogen that was needed as fuel for long-lived stars like the sun, and for making water. For sunlike stars to exist, the ratio of gravity's strength to that of electromagnetism may also have required tuning to one part in many million.

(d) Minor meddling with another nuclear force, the nuclear strong force, or with Planck's constant, which controls the size of the quantum "packets" in which energy is transferred, or with the masses of the neutron and the proton, would have led to a universe without chemistry, made stars burn immensely faster or else not at all, or turned even small objects into neutron stars.

(e) Slight strengthening of electromagnetism would have rendered chemical changes extremely slow, or made hydrogen the only element, or caused all matter to be violently radioactive. It could even have destroyed all atoms.

(f) Various superheavy particles, common early in the Big Bang, needed to have masses falling inside narrow limits. Otherwise there would have been vastly much matter, quickly clumping to form black holes, or else hardly any matter, collisions between particles and antiparticles changing almost all of it into light.

In *Universes* I looked at these and many other such claims. Certainly some of them could be wrong. It is often held, for instance, that the life-permitting expansion speed and the immense smoothness were not fine-tunable. They were instead guaranteed by "inflation," a sudden speeding up of the expansion at early instants. Some people consider that any inflationary mechanism would itself need very accurate tuning, but others don't.

What can look impressive, though, is that so many of the claims appear defensible. It can seem more than a little odd to reject them one and all, perhaps adding that everything was firmly dictated by yet-to-be-discovered principles. (Imagine being invited to watch a computer as it calculates – at any rate that's what you're told – the successive digits of *pi*, the ratio of a circle's circumference to its diameter. After watching much apparent rubbish like 95812240337658964254207 arrive on the computer screen, you suddenly see a long string of ones, twos, and zeros. Translated into Morse-code dots, dashes, and spaces, these spell out GOD WANTED INTELLIGENT LIFE TO EVOLVE. Which is more reasonable: (*i*) telling yourself that those ones, twos, and zeros were mathematically dictated elements of the number *pi*, and so were in no way fine-tunable, or (*ii*) suspecting the existence of a computer-programming prankster?)

Philosophical Attempts to Shrug Off the Fine-Tuning

(1) People often protest that it is arbitrary to pick on *life*, or even *intelligent life*, as something that calls for explanation. Consider dia-monds, which are crystallized carbon. Fred Hoyle drew attention to the accuracy of tuning required if stars were to create carbon in quantity so that carbon-based intelligent organisms like ourselves could in due course make their appearance. Yet why didn't he talk of "diamond-generating tuning" rather than tuning for carbon-based intelligence?

Think of card hands in Bridge. Every hand you could get would be equally improbable, supposing that no cheating were involved, and the likelihood of cheating could seem fairly low. Imagine, however, that you are playing for a million dollars. Somebody gets 13 spades, a hand fine-tuned for success in Bridge. On this evidence, the presence of a cardsharper can appear rather plausible. Now, there could be reasons for thinking that *intelligent life* had the same sort of special status as *hand of 13 spades*. Believers in a divine person, for instance, could have grounds for suspecting that he would not want a lifeless universe.

(2) Another criticism is that the alleged tuning would be beneficial only to life as we know it. Evolving in an arsenic-rich environment, might not arsenic-eating beings speak (equally inappropriately) of "tuning for arsenic"?

A short answer is that considerable tuning could be needed to get either arsenic or anything else that might conceivably support intelligent life. People sometimes suggest that such life can be found in frozen hydrogen or on neutron star surfaces or inside the sun. Inviting us to take this seriously, they treat talk of fine-tuning as nonsense! But since when has getting a universe of frozen hydrogen, neutron stars, suns, been an entirely trivial matter? Far more likely, it could seem, would be a universe of very cold, very dilute gases, or one consisting only of black holes, or one of light rays and little else.

(3) A prerequisite of being puzzled by an intelligent-life-permitting universe is that you are yourself an instance of intelligent life. But as mentioned earlier, the fact that puzzlement's prerequisites have been fulfilled can itself be puzzling. If the 50 sharpshooters of the firing squad all missed you, wouldn't you suspect you were popular with them? – instead of shrugging the matter off by declaring that you'd not be there to puzzle about anything, had any of the bullets hit.

(4) Some maintain that of course our universe cannot be in any way "improbable." Probabilities involve repetitions, they say, whereas the universe is something unique. However, their reasoning fails on numerous fronts. To begin with, why be so sure that our universe is unique? Multiple-universe scenarios are common in such journals as *Physical Review D* and in books you will find in any good public library. Next, even if our universe were the one and only universe, it could still be nonunique among things that seemed in special need of explanation. (A thing can fall into several categories, obviously, and since when has being unique in one category implied being unique in all?) What if the laws of physics made every large cliff bear the words ALLAH CREATED EVERYTHING, or the Buddhist scriptures? "There isn't a huge range of universes inside which ours would be unusual" and "We haven't seen other universes, so how can we judge whether ours is unusual?" would be weird reactions. If you could actually visit enormously many universes,

discovering the message-bearing cliffs in every one of them, would that prove there was nothing mysterious here?

(5) "But can we survey all conceivable laws of physics, plus all imaginable values of cosmically important parameters, so as to find just how many possible universes would include intelligent life?" – Of course we cannot, yet since when have we needed to? We need consider only universes "in the local area of possibilities," universes whose properties are much like those familiar to us, but that have been tuned slightly differently. Imagine that a fly on a wall is hit by a bullet. In a fairly large area surrounding the fly there are no other objects. A natural suspicion can be that the bullet came from a marksman's rifle. Whether there are hugely many other flies outside our fly's "local area" of the wall, or on completely different walls, simply is not relevant.

Multiple Universes and Observational Selection

The story of the fly does, however, suggest a way of avoiding belief in some universe-selecting Marksman. What if the wall is being hit by thousands of bullets? The fact that one of them hits the fly may not be much evidence of marksmanship. Similarly: if there exist hugely many universes differing widely in their properties, it may be no surprise that a few have life-permitting properties. And where could we living beings find ourselves, if not inside one of those few?

Various philosophers protest that a large supply of universes couldn't make it any more probable that any particular universe was life-permitting. Throwing 10 dice a million times doesn't make you more likely to get ten 6s on your very next throw. However, they are overlooking something crucial. Sure enough, beings in a universe that chanced to be life-permitting might rightly view themselves as *immensely lucky* to have come to exist. For perhaps their universe was life-permitting only thanks to how the strengths of physical forces and the masses of elementary particles had become tuned in immensely improbable ways during (here let us get technical for a moment) early symmetry-breaking phase transitions that were influenced by randomly varying scalar fields. But given sufficiently many universes there would almost surely be some in which luck as immense as theirs would be had. Only in those universes would there be physicists asking whether they had been lucky. Their luck would now be *no mystery*. For remember, not only (*i*) would it be unmysterious that living beings were having such good fortune somewhere, but also (*ii*) there *couldn't* be any who discovered they *didn't* have it.

Now, several plausible mechanisms have been suggested for splitting the cosmos into many gigantic domains that could deserve the name of "universes" through being largely or entirely separate from one another, and because of having markedly different properties. Any fine-tuning might be viewed as evidence that at least one such mechanism had been active. Fine-tuned force strengths, particle masses, etc., could in this case suggest *observational selection* instead of divine selection. For as Brandon Carter noted in the early 1970s (see Leslie, ed., 1990), the universe which we observe must in fact – since we are living organisms and not immaterial angels – be a universe which isn't utterly hostile to organically based observership. This is Carter's "strong anthropic principle."

What Observational Selection Maybe Couldn't Make Unmysterious

There may be two things, though, on which observational selection could throw no light.

(A) A physical force strength or a particle mass often appears to need tuning for many different reasons at once. Take electromagnetism. Its strength seemingly calls for tuning, sometimes with immense precision, *first* (a point noted by John Barrow and Frank Tipler) for there to be any marked distinction between matter, from which you can make living beings, and radiation from which you can't; *second* so that quarks wouldn't all be converted into leptons, meaning that there would never have been any atoms; *third* so that protons wouldn't decay so swiftly that there'd soon be no atoms remaining, let alone any organisms able to survive the radiation coming from the decays; *fourth* for protons not to repel one another so strongly that there'd be no such subject as chemistry, and hence no chemically based beings like ourselves; *fifth* for chemical changes to occur speedily enough for life's purposes (a strength increase of even one percent would halve the speed); *sixth* for there to be stars like our sun, burning calmly throughout billions of years and producing light which is not concentrated in the violently destructive ultraviolet range; *seventh* for stellar nucleosynthesis to produce carbon in quantity, and for the carbon to avoid being almost all converted into oxygen (carbon is unique in the number and complexity of its compounds, and is essential to all known organisms); *eighth* for there to be stellar explosions scattering the carbon so that life-forms can be made from it; etc. Well, how came the laws of physics to be such that all these potentially conflicting requirements are satisfied simultaneously?

Why, that is to say, didn't electromagnetism need to be tuned in one way to get stars to generate light of suitable kinds for suitably many years, in a different way for there to be carbon-scattering stellar explosions, in a third way for matter not to be violently radioactive, and so forth? This does not seem a problem solvable by chance variations between immensely many cosmic domains, all obeying the same basic laws of physics but with (for instance) randomly varying scalar fields that tuned force strengths and particle masses differently from one domain to another. For the problem is why those laws made room for even a single life-permitting combination of strengths and of masses.

It could seem, in effect, that what was needed was that the cosmic domains should obey *so many different basic laws of physics* that sooner or later, somewhere, there would be laws which made room for some life-permitting combination. But the idea *that basic laws differ from place to place* can seem something no scientist should rush to accept. It can appear too much in conflict with respect for Induction, the principle that what we have found wherever we have looked is a guide to what should be expected elsewhere. It can seem a step toward saying that Nature is in some regions ruled by magic spells and little blue devils.

(B) Look next at the general form of the laws, disregarding any need to tune various numbers (force strengths, particle masses, and so on). Here again, the same conclusion suggests itself. For making our life-permitting world unmysterious, observational selection can seem far from sufficient.

Take the laws of relativity theory. Regardless, Einstein tells us, of whether a system travels at high speed relative to other systems, observers inside it will find that electromagnetism (which underlies all chemistry) acts equally powerfully in all directions. North–south or east–west, this force tugs exactly as strongly, always, so that (for instance) the delicate operation of the genetic code is never impaired. How can this be true when the force travels not infinitely fast, but only at the velocity of light? Well, light moves always at the same speed relative to a system, as measured from inside that system; hence no matter whether two living organisms are in very rapid motion relative to each other, the internal workings of each can proceed smoothly. Planets, too, are never disturbed by massive earthquakes simply because they rotate, for their gravity (another force transmitted at the speed of light) has no "strongest direction of pull." Beings never find they can see only to the right, light rays coming from the left proving unable to catch up with them. Had such affairs been different, complex life could presumably never have evolved. Yet it could be odd to suppose that Einsteinian relativity operates only in particular regions inside a gigantic cosmos, ones which become observationally selected because observers could never evolve elsewhere.

Much the same can be thought of the laws of quantum theory. Without them, particles would wander around fantastically, as Richard Feynman showed. By preventing electrons from spiraling into atomic nuclei, they allow atoms to exist. They explain why atoms come in many different types, each with properties firmly enough fixed for organisms to be able to rely on them. In short, they are crucial not only to physics but also to physiology. Yet it could be strange to look on them as laws selected observationally, laws perhaps without authority at most times and places.

Observational Selection in Pantheism's Cosmos

What moral comes out of all this? That observational selection is useless for explaining what we find? That our universe's life-permitting character must be attributed to divine selection instead?

In fact the situation is rather more interesting. Yes, if we leave God out of the picture then our universe's life-permitting character can appear an utter mystery. As just now discussed, it can appear to depend on basic laws of physics that are dramatically suitable, and in God's absence there could look to be no plausible way in which such laws could vary from place to place, observational selection then picking out the regions that were life-permitting. However, belief in God can come to the rescue of observational selection – but only if what is in question is the God of pantheism.

There are theologians who disagree with this. Rejecting pantheism, they imagine God as a divine person who creates other beings all infinitely inferior to himself. And they next picture him producing many universes totally hostile to life, for the sheer delight of watching them, observational selection then ensuring that we do not find ourselves in one such universe. Their position, though, can look altogether too strange. For if contemplating all that was worth contemplating, why ever would a divine individual create anything except other divine individuals with the same desirable characteristic? Why would he need to create – not as a pattern of his own thinking but as something external to himself – many a lifeless universe "for the delight of watching it"? Why not just contemplate such universes "in his mind's eye"?

To pantheists, in contrast, universes can be simply divine thought-patterns. And divine thinking extends, they could well believe, not just to universes that are life-containing. It stretches also to others which are firmly life-excluding yet still of great interest, very much worth contemplating. It might stretch even to ones whose basic laws differed in innumerable ways.

The situation is therefore as follows. The fine-tuning, together with the life-permitting nature of the basic laws of physics, probably cannot be understood without something with some right to be called *belief in God*. However, perhaps only pantheism can make such belief at all plausible. Now, when God is pictured pantheistically there can be plenty of room for universes that are utterly hostile to life – and therefore also for observational selection of those that are life-permitting in their laws and in how they are tuned.

Conclusions

It does seem that belief in God could find support in (*a*) the fact that ours is a life-permitting universe, (*b*) the fact that it has causal orderliness, and (*c*) the sheer truth that it is a case of there being "something rather than nothing": something more than a Platonic realm of truths about possibilities. Admittedly, some widely admired theories about God may be so unsatisfactory that no such support could save them. They explain the world's presence by pointing to a divine person whose existence and powers are said to be reasonless. They attribute the world's causal orderliness to planning by a divine mind whose own orderliness is pictured as having no explanation. And they portray divine omnipotence as employed very oddly. The divine person, it is said, could have created other beings with properties just like his own or else almost as marvelous, such as the property of knowing virtually everything he knew. Yet instead he produced – outside himself – crowds of vastly inferior beings. All this can be hard to accept. The combination of Platonism and pantheism, however, could offer us something more plausible. Pantheism puts us *inside* a divine mind, Platonism then giving a reason for that mind's existence. Our world's reality, its causal patterns, its life-permitting character, might all be rather tidily explained when God's existence was treated in something like Spinoza's fashion. This can strengthen the conviction that these things do call for explanation rather than being matters of happenstance.

Now, if such things really could be explained on Platonic and Spinozistic lines then this might well mean – see the previous chapter's arguments – that intelligent living beings were immortal in three distinct ways. When God is not viewed as a Being whose own existence and power are utterly reasonless, even an afterlife can be plausible.

Postscript

It is sometimes protested that a pantheistic scheme of things would be far too grand to include our unsatisfactory universe. This universe could be worth having if nothing else existed. If, however, divine knowledge extended to everything that is superbly wonderful – to knowledge of all beautiful mathematics, for instance, and of all possible fine music, and of the structure of many a universe superior to ours – then no divine mind would go out of its way to contemplate our galaxies, our planets and our depressing selves. The idea that humans and their surroundings are nothing but elements in divine thought is absurd, for ethical reasons. They are too second-rate! They'd too much dilute all the really good stuff.

In *The End of the World* I discussed all manner of threats to human survival. Some would come from bad philosophy if people ever listened to philosophers. I considered Schopenhauer's argument that humans are fated to be more miserable than happy since they think hardly ever of their blessings, almost always of "the one spot where the shoe pinches," and that therefore Earth "would better have remained like the moon, a lifeless mass." In addition I looked at the doctrine that since human life has already included much happiness its continuation into future centuries would be worthless or worse than worthless. Here one suggestion is that the good of there being happy lives must somehow reach a limit whereas the evil of there being miserable ones keeps growing with each new unhappy person – so that, while a single island inhabited by a million happy people plus two or three who were miserable could be something good, some huge number of islands precisely like it would be extremely evil! These and other reasons for encouraging human extinction are currently defended by many philosophers, I reported. They struck me as rather poor reasons.

The idea that the world we inhabit would not merit a divine mind's contemplation, such a mind having other more marvelous things to contemplate, strikes me as equally poor. Suppose you were convinced that our intricately structured universe exists inside an intricately structured mind, a mind contemplating everything that can be conceived without contradiction. (Let us say you joined Richard Swinburne in arguing that an omniscient mind would be something of a particularly simple kind and therefore quite to be expected.) Suppose also that you believed you could delete the universe by wiping out the divine thoughts about it, after first deleting everything inferior to it. Would you conclude *that you ought to*? That, just because many finer things were being contemplated, it would be right to annihilate all of us? Let's hope not! Let's hope you would think our universe worth contemplating *as well*.

If its intelligent living beings were immortal in one or more ways, it could be all the more worth contemplating.

Further Reading

I introduced this chapter's themes in *Value and Existence*, in *Universes*, in *Infinite Minds*, and in articles going back to "The Theory that the World Exists Because It Should" in the October 1970 issue of the *American Philosophical Quarterly*. For passages often interpreted as an outright dismissal of the need to explain the world's existence and its causal orderliness, see Hume's *A Treatise of Human Nature* or his *Enquiry concerning Human Understanding*. In the *Critique of Pure Reason*, however, Kant can be viewed as developing a point taken straight from Hume, namely, that experience could teach us nothing unless guided by such principles as "Things don't exist reasonlessly" and "Events never reasonlessly exhibit regularities." A careful reading of Hume's *Dialogues concerning Natural*

Religion shows that Hume hesitated about treating life as "only natural" in a way that would have left nothing for Darwin to explain.

Leibniz's *The Ultimate Origin of Things*, a short paper he dated 23 November, 1697, is highly recommended. Although Swinburne's *The Existence of God* and *The Coherence of Theism* are also much recommended, it may be hard to accept their argument that an infinite, omnipotent person would be a reality of a specially simple kind, and thus quite to be expected despite existing reasonlessly. For Ayer's suggestion that "doing better than chance" could prove nothing in card-guessing experiments, see chapter 7 of his *Metaphysics and Common Sense*.

On cosmic fine-tuning and multiple universes, consult Barrow, Barrow & Tipler, Davies, Ellis, Polkinghorne, and Rees: relevant works of theirs are given in the Bibliography. I list many further writings on these topics in *Universes* and in my edited volume *Modern Cosmology and Philosophy*. This contains discussions of it by Swinburne, by Brandon Carter, by Bernard Carr, and by George Gale, as well as reprinting a survey article of my own, "The Anthropic Principle Today."

APPENDIX: BRIEF
SUMMARY OF THE BOOK

Immortality Defended develops a creation story told by Plato. The reason why there is anything actually in existence – anything beyond a realm of truths about mere possibilities – is that this is good. A divine being perhaps, or maybe the entire cosmos, exists just because of an ethical requirement. Although logic could never prove it, the requirement has a creative success that is necessary in an absolute fashion. What gives it the success? Nothing. Compare how no cogwheels, magnetic fields, or magic spells "give" misery its ability to be necessarily worse than happiness.

On such a theory, why is there anything apart from infinite divine awareness of everything worth thinking about? Well, maybe there exists nothing else, as Spinoza and other pantheists recognize. All the things of our universe could exist just in the intricately structured thinking of a single mind, perhaps well worth calling "divine." Without our knowing it, the patterns of our lives would be mere ingredients of its thought-patterns.

The various parts of any such mind would be united in a fashion familiar to quantum physicists, and to everybody whenever conscious of many things all at once. Like the color, length, and shape of a brick, the parts would not be real each in isolation from the others. But despite being unified in its existence, a single cosmic whole, the divine mind could include countless universes in addition to ours.

It could include, too, many things not organized into universes, and we might even come to experience them. When our bodies had died we should presumably be in existence "back there along the fourth dimension" as Einstein thought, which would make us in some interesting sense immortal, but we could have the immortality of an afterlife as well. Our experiences could continue onwards indefinitely, giving us an ever-increasing share of the wonders of infinite thought. This might be miraculous, but not in the sense of making natural laws break down in the world we had known previously.

Suppose, however, that both "Einsteinian immortality" and an afterlife were fictions. We should still have immortality of a third type for which people have sometimes hoped. The divine mind that had lived our lives as tiny elements of its thinking would continue to exist for ever.

If Plato were correct in his explanation of why things exist, then reality would presumably consist not just of one infinite mind, but of infinitely many, because this would be best. All the same, the situation would not be so perfect that the ethical need for one thing never clashed with the ethical need for another. There would be plenty of room for us to reduce such conflict, improving our tiny segment of the cosmos. Pantheism, the belief that nothing exists except divine thinking, in no way denies all the obvious facts recognized by science and by common sense, one of them being that our efforts can affect the world well or badly. Yet although such facts are evident, the world around them may strike us as mysterious. Both science and common sense can see problems – Why is there any world at all? Why does our world obey any laws, let alone life-permitting ones? Why does our cosmic environment seem fine-tuned for the evolution of intelligent organisms? – which Platonism and pantheism can venture to answer. If the answers are judged satisfactory, our chances of having all three kinds of immortality can seem high.

BIBLIOGRAPHY

Ayer, A. J. (1970). *Metaphysics and Common Sense*. San Francisco: Freeman, Cooper.

Barrow, J. D. (2001). "Cosmology, Life and the Anthropic Principle." In James B. Miller (ed.), *Cosmic Questions*, pp. 139–53. New York: New York Academy of Sciences.

—— (2002). *The Constants of Nature*. London: Jonathan Cape.

—— and F. J. Tipler (1986). *The Anthropic Cosmological Principle*. Oxford: Clarendon Press.

Bohm, D., and B. J. Hiley (1993). *The Undivided Universe*. London and New York: Routledge.

Bradley, F. H. (1893). *Appearance and Reality*. London: Oxford University Press.

—— (1914). *Essays on Truth and Reality*. London: Oxford University Press.

—— (1935). *Collected Essays: Volume Two*. London: Oxford University Press.

Broad, C. D. (1925). *The Mind and its Place in Nature*. London: Routledge and Kegan Paul.

Clayton, P., and A. Peacocke (eds.) (2004). *In Whom We Live and Move and Have Our Being*. Grand Rapids, MI: William B. Eerdmans.

Davies, P. C. W. (1980). *Other Worlds*. London: Dent.

—— (1982). *The Accidental Universe*. Cambridge: Cambridge University Press.

Deutsch, D. (1997). *The Fabric of Reality*. London: Allen Lane.

Eddington, A. S. (1928). *The Nature of the Physical World*. Cambridge: Cambridge University Press.

Edwards, P. (ed.) (1992). *Immortality*. New York: Macmillan.

Einstein, A. (1962). *Relativity: The Special and the General Theory* (15th ed., enlarged). London: Methuen.

Ellis, G. F. R. (1993). *Before the Beginning*. London: Bowerdean Press.

Ewing, A. C. (1973). *Value and Reality*. London: George Allen and Unwin.

Forrest, P. (1996). *God without the Supernatural*. Ithaca and London: Cornell University Press.

Fröhlich, H., and F. Kremer (eds.) (1983). *Coherent Excitations in Biological Systems*. Berlin: Springer-Verlag.

Grünbaum, A. (1967). "The Status of Temporal Becoming." In R. M. Gale (ed.), *The Philosophy of Time*, pp. 322–53. Garden City, NY: Doubleday.

—— (1973). *Philosophical Problems of Space and Time* (2nd ed.). Dordrecht and Boston: Reidel.

Hameroff, S. R. (1994). "Quantum Coherence in Microtubules: A Neural Basis for Emergent Consciousness?" *Journal of Consciousness Studies*, 1(1): 91–118.

James, W. (1890). *The Principles of Psychology: Volume One*. New York: Henry Holt.

Jeans, J. (1930). *The Mysterious Universe*. London: Macmillan.

King-Farlow, J. (1978). *Self-Knowledge and Social Relations*. New York: Science History Publications.

Küng, H. (1980). *Does God Exist?* London: Collins.

Leslie, J. (1979). *Value and Existence*. Oxford: Blackwell, and Lanham, MD: Rowman and Littlefield.

—— (1989). *Universes*. London and New York: Routledge. Paperback edition, slightly rev., 1996.

—— (ed.) (1990). *Physical Cosmology and Philosophy*. New York: Macmillan. Expanded ed. from Prometheus Books, Amherst, NY, as *Modern Cosmology and Philosophy* (1998).

—— (1996). *The End of the World: The Science and Ethics of Human Extinction*. London and New York: Routledge. Paperback ed., slightly revised and with new Preface, 1998.

—— (2001). *Infinite Minds*. Oxford and New York: Oxford University Press. Paperback ed. 2003.

Lewis, D. (1986). *On the Plurality of Worlds*. Oxford: Blackwell.

Lockwood, M. (1989). *Mind, Brain and the Quantum*. Oxford: Blackwell.

Mackie, J. L. (1972). *Problems from Locke*. Oxford: Oxford University Press.

—— (1977). *Ethics: Inventing Right and Wrong*. Harmondsworth: Penguin Books.

—— (1982). *The Miracle of Theism*. Oxford: Oxford University Press.

Marshall, I. N. (1989). "Consciousness and Bose–Einstein Condensates." *New Ideas in Psychology*, 7(1): 73–83.

McTaggart, J. M. E. (1927). *The Nature of Existence*, ed. C. D. Broad. Cambridge: Cambridge University Press.

Nagel, T. (1979). *Mortal Questions.* Cambridge: Cambridge University Press.

Nozick, R. (1989). *The Examined Life.* New York: Simon and Schuster.

Parfit, D. (1992). "The Puzzle of Reality." *The Times Literary Supplement,* July 3: 3–5.

—— (1998). "Why Anything? Why This?," a two-part article in *London Review of Books,* Jan. 27: 24–7, and Feb. 5: 22–5.

Penrose, R. (1987). "Minds, Machines and Mathematics," in C. Blakemore and S. Greenfield (eds.), *Mindwaves,* pp. 259–76. Oxford: Blackwell.

—— (1989). *The Emperor's New Mind.* Oxford: Oxford University Press.

—— (1994). *Shadows of the Mind.* Oxford: Oxford University Press.

Penrose, R., with A. Shimony, N. Cartwright, S. Hawking, and N. Longair (1997). *The Large, the Small and the Human Mind.* Cambridge: Cambridge University Press.

Polkinghorne, J. (1986). *One World: The Interaction of Science and Theology.* Princeton: Princeton University Press.

—— (1994). *The Faith of a Physicist.* Princeton: Princeton University Press.

Redhead, M. (1995). *From Physics to Metaphysics.* Cambridge: Cambridge University Press.

Rees, M. J. (1997). *Before the Beginning: Our Universe and Others.* Reading, MA: Addison-Wesley.

—— (2000). *Just Six Numbers.* New York: Basic Books.

—— (2001). *Our Cosmic Habitat.* Princeton: Princeton University Press.

—— (2003). *Our Final Century.* London: William Heinemann.

Rescher, N. (1984). *The Riddle of Existence.* Lanham, MD, and London: University Press of America.

—— (2000). *Nature and Understanding.* Oxford: Oxford University Press.

Rice, H. (2000). *God and Goodness.* Oxford: Oxford University Press.

Russell, B. (1903). *Principles of Mathematics.* Cambridge: Cambridge University Press.

—— (1914). *Our Knowledge of the External World.* Chicago: Open Court.

—— (1927). *The Analysis of Matter.* London: Kegan Paul.

Schrödinger, E. (1958). *Mind and Matter.* Cambridge: Cambridge University Press.

—— (1964). *My View of the World.* Cambridge: Cambridge University Press.

Seager, W. (1999). *Theories of Consciousness.* London and New York: Routledge.

Searle, J. R. (1984). *Minds, Brains and Science,* Reith Lectures published in *The Listener.*

—— (1997). *The Mystery of Consciousness.* London: Granta Books.

Shimony, A. (1988). "The Reality of the Quantum World." *Scientific American,* Jan.: 46–53.

—— (1997). "On Mentality, Quantum Mechanics and the Actualization of Potentialities," in R. Penrose et al., *The Large, the Small and the Human Mind*, pp. 144–69. Cambridge: Cambridge University Press.

Shoemaker, S. (1969). "Time without Change." *Journal of Philosophy*, June 19: 363–81.

Smart, J. J. C. (1967). "Time," in P. Edwards (ed.), *The Encyclopedia of Philosophy: Volume Seven*, pp. 126–34. New York: Macmillan Publishing and The Free Press.

—— (1989). *Our Place in the Universe*. Oxford: Blackwell.

Smolin, L. (1997). *The Life of the Cosmos*. London: Weidenfeld and Nicolson.

Sprigge, T. L. S. (1983). *The Vindication of Absolute Idealism*. Edinburgh: Edinburgh University Press.

—— (1984). *Theories of Existence*. Harmondsworth: Penguin Books.

Swinburne, R. (1977). *The Coherence of Theism*. Oxford: Oxford University Press.

—— (1979). *The Existence of God*. Oxford: Oxford University Press.

Tillich, P. (1953–63). *Systematic Theology*. London: Nisbet.

Ward, K. (1996). *Religion and Creation*. Oxford: Oxford University Press.

—— (2006). *Pascal's Fire*. Oxford: OneWorld.

Weinberg, S. (1993). *Dreams of a Final Theory*. London: Hutchinson.

Whitehead, A. N. (1978). *Process and Reality*, corrected ed. New York: Macmillan.

Williams, D. C. (1951). "The Myth of Passage," in the *Journal of Philosophy*; reprinted in R. M. Gale (ed.) (1967), *The Philosophy of Time*, pp. 98–116. Garden City: Doubleday.

Zohar, D. (1996). "Consciousness and Bose-Einstein Condensates," in S. R. Hameroff, A. W. Kaszniak, and A. C. Scott (eds.), *Towards a Science of Consciousness*, pp. 430–50. Cambridge, MA: MIT Press.

INDEX OF NAMES

INDEX OF SUBJECTS